CANADABIS

The Canadian Weed Reader

E. Reid Ross

Adams Media

New York London Toronto Sydney New Delhi

A **adams**media

Adams Media
An Imprint of Simon & Schuster, Inc.
57 Littlefield Street
Avon, Massachusetts 02322

First Adams Media trade paperback edition OCTOBER 2017

ADAMS MEDIA and colophon are trademarks of Simon and Schuster.

For information about special discounts for bulk purchases, please contact Simon & Schuster Special Sales at 1-866-506-1949 or business@simonandschuster.com.

The Simon & Schuster Speakers Bureau can bring authors to your live event. For more information or to book an event contact the Simon & Schuster Speakers Bureau at 1-866-248-3049 or visit our website at www.simonspeakers.com.

Interior design by Colleen Cunningham

Interior image © Getty Images

Manufactured in the United States of America

10 9 8 7 6 5 4 3 2

Library of Congress Cataloging-in-Publication Data has been applied for.

ISBN 978-1-5072-0584-6
ISBN 978-1-5072-0591-4 (ebook)

Contains material adapted from the following titles published by Adams Media, an Imprint of Simon & Schuster, Inc.: *Weed* by I.M. Stoned, copyright © 2009, ISBN 978-1-4405-0349-8; *Weed 2016 Daily Calendar* by I.M. Stoned, copyright © 2015, ISBN 978-1-4405-8857-0; and *Weed 2017 Daily Calendar* by I.M. Stoned, copyright © 2016, ISBN 978-1-4405-9818-0.

CONTENTS

INTRODUCTION

Canada and cannabis have an interesting history together. While Canadian marijuana has long been highly prized for its quality, until recently it's been highly illegal to grow or possess. To arm those who weren't thoroughly prepared for the sudden influx of weed into their lives, we've assembled exactly four hundred and twenty (a number that is near and dear to every pot enthusiast) factual tidbits, informative quotes, and funny stories about marijuana so that readers might be properly armed for this wonderful cultural shift. We will explain some of the great connections our great land has with weed, look at some of the science and studies behind the plant, meet some other stoners you may have heard of, and more. And for those who already include pot consumption among their list of favorite things to do, there's a lot of information here that you've probably forgotten.

ONE

MARIJUANA IN THE GREAT WHITE NORTH

Canada is one of the most unique countries for fans of weed. With ample land to grow on and many hardworking marijuana activists, Canada has quickly become one of the world's best places to live the stoner life. Now that weed is legal, Canucks are making their love of Mary Jane known more than ever. Here are some facts that prove that Canada is truly home to that magical leaf.

CANADA IS HOME TO
THE BIGGEST
GREENHOUSE ON EARTH

1

The medical marijuana greenhouse in Niagara-on-the-Lake, Ontario, sprawls out at 350,000 square feet and is "blanketed in security systems and everything from sanitation to production is tightly regulated." So there go your hopes of impersonating a janitor and sneaking in to spend a month or two living in one of the utility closets.

YOUR
HIGHNESS

2

Marc Emery is Canada's self-anointed "Prince of Pot." As the head of British Columbia's Marijuana Party, he has worked tirelessly for years as an advocate for cannabis rights, while also owning and operating a store in Vancouver that sells "everything from bongs to pot leaf tee shirts." Unfortunately, he was arrested in early 2017 on several drug trafficking charges. He hasn't yet said whether he'll be claiming immunity as royalty.

3 THE TRAGICALLY HEMP?

The Canadian rock band known as the Tragically Hip have positioned themselves strategically in preparation for their retirement from the music scene by forming a partnership with the medical marijuana company called Newstrike. The executive chairman of the company explained the reasoning behind the collaboration thusly: "No one knows Canada and Canadians like the members of the Tragically Hip. With their involvement and support, Newstrike firmly believes we are developing the brand that adult consumers who choose to use cannabis will turn to."

4 SECONDHAND EMBARRASSMENT

The sport of snowboarding made its first Olympic appearance at Nagano in 1998, and Ross Rebagliati did our country proud by bringing home the very first gold. Pride rapidly turned to national disgrace, however, when Rebagliati's medal was taken away after a positive test for marijuana. He claimed that he was merely the victim of a secondhand smoke–filled party, to no avail. But when the Canadian Olympic delegation appealed the decision on the basis that weed shouldn't count as a performance-enhancing drug, they were successful and Rebagliati's medal was returned. Rebagliati later parlayed this fame into a successful medical marijuana company fittingly named "Ross' Gold."

A HARSH
REALITY

A story recently began circulating that Tim Hortons would be getting into the marijuana dispensary business once it was legalized. It was later shown to be from a parody website, proving once again that you can never trust what you read on the Internet.

WE NEED
MORE WEED!

Before the official start date of legal marijuana, the government ran into an interesting problem. Ontario's finance minister, Charles Sousa, said the biggest problem "is one of supply." Apparently demand is so high to get high that an analyst claimed there would be a shortage right away.

7 WILL HE SELL DONUTS TOO?

British Columbia's own pot baron Don Briere used to be Canada's busiest marijuana grower and seller, at one point making $5 million per year on the stuff. Now that weed is legal, he's said that he wants his head shops, Weeds Glass and Gifts, to become "the Tim Hortons of cannabis." Or maybe he wants to make Timmy's "the Weeds of coffee."

8 CALL IT VANSTERDAM

If you have any question as to which way the tides of Canadian history are turning, wrap your head around this: recently the city of Vancouver became home to more marijuana dispensaries than Tim Hortons franchises. Which suggests that the sooner fast food chains incorporate Cheetos-based options in their menus, the better.

9 SHOULD HAVE KEPT IT
ON THE DOWN LOW

When marijuana reform advocates in British Columbia needed a place to hold their meetings, they decided on Tim Hortons restaurants for reasons likely related to their close proximity to muffins and/or donuts. The arrangement worked out just fine for a while, until the activists started announcing the fact in newspapers. The Tims people didn't really care for such a public association, and forced the group to meet elsewhere, much to the likely benefit of all Taco Bells within a 100-mile radius.

10 FIRST IN
THE WORLD

In 2001, Canada became the first country to legalize medical marijuana. After a man named Terry Parker successfully argued that the marijuana laws at the time were unconstitutional, the government began allowing people to grow marijuana for their own personal medical use.

11 BLUNT
HONESTY

While US President Bill Clinton famously claimed to have not inhaled when asked about his past experiences with marijuana, Prime Minister Justin Trudeau is a little more...blunt. He's admitted to inhaling plenty of times, including while he was a member of Parliament, and that he has no regrets about it at all.

12 SECONDS, PLEASE

A new hybrid strain of cannabis, made up of 90 percent indica and 10 percent sativa, called either "Maple Syrup" or "Maple Leaf," should immediately be put in place as the national marijuana strain of the Great White North. Its flavor is exactly as sweet as its name implies and, unsurprisingly, it has a reputation for inducing extreme, near uncontrollable levels of the munchies.

13 JOINT CHIEF

In 2016, Bill Blair, a former Toronto Police chief and an MP, was put in charge of a task force with the goal of making sure marijuana legalization wouldn't cause Canada to become a lawless dystopia. His job, according to a government spokesman, would be to "ensure we keep marijuana out of the hands of children, and the profits out of the hands of criminals." Blair has said he's never tried marijuana before and won't once it's legal, but who knows. It worked out pretty well for the last MP who smoked while in Parliament.

TAKE
TWO

Justin isn't the first Prime Minister Trudeau to be involved with the battle for legal marijuana. In 1969, his father, Pierre Trudeau, brought about the Commission of Inquiry into the Non-Medical Use of Drugs (also known as the Le Dain Commission). Unfortunately, the commission's recommendation to decriminalize the possession and growth of marijuana was ignored at the time. But now the son is finishing what the father started.

CANNABINOID
SAUVIGNON

During a recent conference in Toronto, business leaders discussed strategy for the future of the Canadian economy. One of the suggestions that came up, one that would have been practically unthinkable a decade before, was to make the country a "world leader in the burgeoning marijuana industry." Alan Gertner, the owner of a weed-friendly cafe chain called Tokyo Smoke and attendee of the conference, declared that Canada might one day "be to cannabis what France is to wine." Representatives from the baguette and cheese industries allegedly began to cheer loudly when they heard this.

HOLD YOUR HORSES

Despite Prime Minister Trudeau's "enthusiasm" for marijuana while he was an MP, he's gone on record stating he's no fan whatsoever of those who jumped the gun by flouting the current laws still in place. And when a large number of unlicensed dispensaries began popping up in Toronto before any laws were changed, he described the situation as "frustrating." Or maybe he was just annoyed that the phenomenon wasn't happening in Ottawa.

17 HIGH FINANCE

A mover and shaker in the Canadian marijuana trade, the conveniently named Abi Roach is the owner of the Toronto head shop Roach-o-Rama. She followed that venture with the opening of a marijuana lounge named Hotbox and then began publishing the free magazine *Spliff*, which covers the Ontario cannabis scene. If you're wondering whether these sorts of business activities are good for making a profit, she also owns property in Jamaica where travelers can partake in "weed tourism." Basically, if there's a capitalistic niche that needs filling, Ms. Roach is there— just so long as that niche is loaded with THC.

18 THC MBA

Kwantlen Polytechnic University in Vancouver offers a series of courses in a field that once was dominated solely by enterprising crooks: the business of weed. The "Cannabis Professional Series" includes courses called Plant Production & Facility Management; Marketing, Sales & Drug Development; and Financing a Cannabis Enterprise in Canada. Plus, it can all be taken online. Which is smart, considering the potential paranoia level of the average student taking this course.

19 WE'RE NUMBER ONE!

According to a recent UNICEF survey, young Canadians smoke more marijuana than anyone else in the western world. However, countries with especially lax attitudes on weed, like Holland and Portugal, scored much lower, supporting the idea that legalization actually lowers the rate of drug use—and likely leading to Canada's decline in rankings on the next survey. Then again, when you're dealing with surveys and teenagers, there's always the risk that they're actively yanking your chain.

20 I MEAN, APPARENTLY IT WORKED

A marijuana activist from British Columbia named Dana Larsen devised a unique way of getting the attention of the Liberal members of Parliament before the vote to legalize marijuana—he mailed each of them a gram of pot. Fully aware of the illegality of his actions, he brazenly declared that he had no fear of the police, mostly because he didn't think they'd care. He said, "It's not legal to mail people weed…but most of Canada's marijuana laws are made to be broken, so that's just another one. I don't think any Liberal MP is going to call the police, and if they do I don't think the police are going to come after me for a gram of pot."

THE STONEY
MAJORITY

While a clear majority of Canadians (61 percent) believe that marijuana should be legal, slightly less than half (49 percent) believe that people should be allowed to grow their own pot at home. This might seem puzzling, until you take into account just how lucrative such an endeavor can be. And maybe what they mean is that they don't want anyone *else* growing their own weed.

PROVINCIAL
PUFFERS

If asked to guess which Canadian province smokes the most marijuana per capita, most people would probably guess it was British Columbia. But nope! According to a recent survey, it's Nova Scotia with 14.8 percent of their citizens smoking the reefer.

23 IT DOESN'T WORK
AS WELL FOR NAUSEA

Using the medical profession to get "legal" marijuana actually has a precedent. In the early twentieth century, when the provinces (and eventually all of Canada) began banning the sale of alcohol, people would have a doctor prescribe "medicinal whiskey" to get their hands on liquor.

24 WON'T SOMEONE THINK
OF THE CHILDREN?

Not everyone in Canada is all aboard on the marijuana-legalization train. Former Conservative leadership candidate Kellie Leitch stated publicly that cannabis is a "dangerous drug," and made a vow that should she ever become prime minister, she would reverse its legalization. As a pediatric orthopedic surgeon, she claimed to be especially concerned about it potentially getting into the hands of children. Which makes one wonder when was the last time she visited a public school.

25 WHAT WOULD JESUS SMOKE?

Before Justin Trudeau came on the scene, hopes for marijuana being a legal commodity in Canada were looking pretty dim. Prime Minister Harper stated unequivocally that he was entirely against the idea. When he was asked whether or not he had ever smoked weed he said he hadn't. "I'm asthmatic," he said. "I cannot smoke and have never smoked anything. In terms of temptation I will leave any comment on that to my dialogue with my maker."

26 I'VE HAD WORSE VACATIONS THAN WINE AND WEED

Canada's very first national video advertisement for the marijuana industry was broadcast recently. With acoustic guitar playing in the background, a narrator lovingly spoke of British Columbia's outdoor recreational opportunities such as mom-and-pop vineyards and farmers markets. Which segued nicely into a discussion of another source of pride for the area: its 17,000 pot farms.

 27 MORE LIKE "GO DIRECTLY TO JAIL"

Apparently the legalization of marijuana in Canada will not result in a "get out of jail free" card for those with previous convictions for possession, even when it was only for carrying small amounts. While many had hoped for a blanket amnesty to take place, the government has stated, "That's not an item that's on the agenda at the moment."

 28 FUGITIVE FARMS

A resort called Whitewater in the small town of Nelson, British Columbia, is one of Canada's best-kept secrets, not just for the pristine slopes that attract skiers and snowboarders, but also for the area's cash crop. The marijuana trade has been booming for decades in this remote locale, since Americans trying to avoid the Vietnam War hid there in the sixties and seventies, bringing with them their excellent vocational ideas.

29 SMOKE SHACK,

Many ski slopes have small wooden structures situated intermittently around the landscape, and one would assume that they're just for taking a break to get warm or eat without having to journey all the way back down to a lodge. But another, unannounced reason someone might duck in is that they're a great place to safely smoke marijuana. Which explains another term skiers and snowboarders have for them: "smoke shacks."

30 "OY!" "EH?"

Ski resorts have a strange phenomenon to deal with every January 26. That date happens to be Australia Day, a national holiday when Aussies descend upon ski towns to do things like dance naked in the snow, drink like there's no tomorrow, and, of course, smoke copious amounts of weed. And with marijuana legalization removing a troublesome impediment to their debauchery, Canadians might consider staying off the slopes on that day—or else be ready for a party.

31 LONG
AWAITED

Canada first outlawed marijuana in 1923 through the Opium and Drug Act. However, the first possession charge didn't come about until 1937. Maybe they forgot they'd outlawed it for fourteen years?

32 NORTHERN
DOMINANCE

Thanks to years of practice, state-of-the-art technology, and advanced weed husbandry methods, Canadian marijuana today is reportedly five times as potent as what was smoked in the 1970s. It's been a multi-billion dollar industry for years and is considered something of a gourmet product among pot enthusiasts. And with legalization, who knows what measures the Mexican cartels will have to resort to in order to keep up. Maybe hiring guys to stand on corners to flip around a giant foam pot leaf or something. That always seems to work.

TWO

THE SCIENCE OF CANNABIS

The study of cannabis has had to overcome many hurdles over the years, in no small part due to many governments treating a simple plant like a vile weed infesting their nation. But as more and more restrictions are lifted and researchers continue to probe the inner workings of the ganja leaf, new medical possibilities (and sobering realities) are being uncovered every day. Here are some of the highlights, past and present, of the scientific world's ongoing fascination with pot.

33 SCHOOL DAZE

According to Ontario's University of Waterloo, just about as many teens smoke weed as smoke cigarettes. And they found that while only 2 percent of kids in seventh to eleventh grades engage in the activity, that number climbs to 5 percent once they hit the twelfth grade. After that, it presumably depends on whether those surveyed live within driving distance of a venue where Tom Petty continues to tour.

34 "YOU'LL FRY YOUR BRAI... NEVER MIND"

Researchers studying marijuana at the University of Saskatchewan reported a surprising discovery. They found that a "synthetic cannabinoid," similar to a substance found in actual marijuana, stimulates cell growth in the brain. As contrary as that sounds to what most kids are told by their mothers while growing up, this finding may be helpful in creating medicines for those suffering from anxiety and depression.

35 IS THERE ANYTHING POT CAN'T CURE?

Adding to the seemingly endless list of medical maladies treatable with medical marijuana, research conducted in 2013 suggests that the drug could help individuals who suffer from the inflammatory bowel disorder known as Crohn's disease. Individuals who participated in the study smoked two joints a day for eight weeks. At the conclusion of the study, half of the subjects reported a complete cessation of their symptoms.

36 MARIJUANA
AND ALZHEIMER'S

A new study has found that the THC in pot may be useful as a treatment for Alzheimer's disease. Specifically, THC stimulates the removal of toxic plaque in the brain, which some scientists believe actually causes Alzheimer's. Researchers are still unsure whether or not the treatment will be useful for humans, but so far there haven't been any complaints from the rats.

37 A FURRY
HIGH

Blowing smoke in your cat's face is a dick move to be sure, not to mention dangerous, but could sick pets benefit from medical marijuana just like their owners? Undeterred by a complete and utter lack of research into the subject, some veterinarians in the US state of California are prescribing cannabis treatments for dogs and cats alike. Reportedly, a month's supply only runs about $40, so it's probably worth a shot, especially if Mittens is looking to expand his mind beyond the limitations of catnip in a sock. Just make sure you have a note from the vet when you try to cross the border back home.

38 THE WORLD'S MOST EXPENSIVE OVERDOSE

Marijuana consumption may not be the healthiest habit in the world, but it's nowhere near as dangerous as many would have you believe. According to various government authorities, you'd have to eat either one-third of your entire body weight or 1,500 pounds of the stuff for the chemical compounds within it to be fatal. We don't recommend you test out which number is more accurate, however, unless you have a whole lot of disposable income and/or are part goat.

39 "PSST...GOT ANY E-WEED?"

You can buy and sell just about anything on the Internet nowadays, whether it's technically legal or not. So maybe it shouldn't come as much of a shock that the very first e-commerce transaction ever was for— you guessed it—weed. In the early 1970s, students at the Stanford Artificial Intelligence Laboratory used a very early version of the Internet to make an illicit deal with some other students at the Massachusetts Institute of Technology for an undetermined amount of marijuana.

40 SMOKING A FATTY

The idea that smoking pot gives you the munchies is a well-worn chestnut, but it turns out there's hard science to back it up. The active ingredient in cannabis (cannabinoids, naturally) manipulates the part of the brain that controls appetite, basically switching off the cells that let you know when you're full. Researchers said it fools the brain's central feeding system, and "it's like pressing a car's brakes and accelerating instead."

41 THC IQ

A recent study from the United Kingdom (conducted at Cardiff University in Wales) showed people with higher IQs tended toward dabbling in marijuana, as well as other drugs. And another recent British study from University College London soundly debunked the frequent claims that heavy pot smoking in adolescence makes you dumber. So why aren't McGill and UofT scouring the nation's high-school bathrooms and public playgrounds after dark for the next generation of hotshot astrophysicists?

42 BLAME SOCIETY!

According to new research, people who act like stupid stoners may be doing so not because of any effects marijuana may be having on their brains, but simply because they are subconsciously matching society's expectations of how a person who frequently gets high should behave. And, according to the study, this phenomenon may be particularly pronounced in males. If you actually do happen to be a stupid stoner, however, pay this no mind. You just keep on being you, champ.

43 DOGGY DAZE

With the rise of marijuana use comes the rise of dim-wits who either can't figure out how to store their pot in a safe place or think it's just hilarious to get their pets baked. A veterinary study in Colorado reported a 400 percent increase in the number of calls they received about the family dog becoming dangerously intoxicated on cheeba after the state legalized medical marijuana. Unless your vet gave Spot a prescription, don't feed your pets any drugs. Come on, people.

44 WHY WOULD YOU GIVE A SPIDER THE MUNCHIES?

Intrepid scientists are always looking to unlock the secrets of the natural world, which seems like a pretty flimsy excuse for the fact that somebody conducted research on how well spiders build their webs while high. This vitally important work began in 1948 by a German biologist named H.M. Peters. When he forced some arachnids to ingest marijuana, their building skills became...well...the best word would probably be "haphazard."

45 WEE FOR YOUR WEED

Growing experts have advised that peeing on your marijuana plants is a great way to "infuse a little nitrogen" into your crop. Not to mention phosphorus and potassium, which are both very common in urine and vital nutrients for every growing bud. Well, actually, you shouldn't urinate directly onto the poor little guys. It's recommended you dilute it a bit with water. But if you're dead set on peeing on your garden (for reasons that can remain your own), maybe you can just chug a bunch of water beforehand?

46 AIRBORNE CHRONIC

Trees Delivery, a marijuana-delivery business based out of San Francisco, plans to incorporate the latest technology by sending out subscribers' weed via drones. According to CEO Marshall Hayner, "We see drones as an amazing tool for delivery. A drone will never be late." At least if a delivery does happen to be late, angry stoners will be much less likely to verbally abuse a flying robot.

47 GANJA GUPPIES

If you like weed and like staring at fish, did you know you can combine those things in the weirdest way possible? Aquaponics (the combination of aquaculture and hydroponics) is a system that allows you to grow marijuana while also providing an environment for fish, snails, turtles, giant squid...whatever you want—depending on the size of your tank, of course.

48 NIGHT TOKER

Can marijuana actually improve your night vision? Research seems to suggest that very well could be the case. It apparently makes retinal cells more sensitive to light, which could explain the mystery of the Jamaican fishermen who have an "uncanny ability to see in the dark" after smoking it or gobbling it down with rum. This isn't something we just made up, but an actual observation made by a scientist nearly thirty years ago.

 SMOKY PALPITATIONS

Don't let Willie Nelson's uncanny longevity fool you into thinking you can smoke like a fiend into middle age and suffer no ill effects. While it's certainly safer overall than smoking cigarettes, a study by Boston's Beth Israel Deaconess Medical Center and Harvard Medical School found inhaling marijuana may give you a 500 percent greater chance than nonsmokers of having a heart attack within the first hour of lighting up. And age increases the risk, so once your hair starts turning gray, you may want to start baking brownies instead.

 A PICTURE'S WORTH A THOUSAND TOKES

Scientists at China's ShanghaiTech University were recently able to create a 3D representation of the human molecular structure activated by the active ingredient in cannabis, THC, for the first time ever. Reportedly, the discovery "advances the understanding of how marijuana works in the human body," and will hopefully lead to even stronger weed.

TEEN TOKERS

An old trope that every teenager has heard for decades is how smoking marijuana in your youth can lead to health problems down the road. Well, a recent study from the University of Pittsburgh Medical Center appears to alleviate or downright debunk a good portion of those concerns. The research found that smoking pot as an adolescent really doesn't have much of an effect whatsoever on *any* mental or physical health problems that they could find. Well, unless you're the sort that enjoys drinking bong water. Then you're probably just asking for the reaper to make you a priority case.

DIRTY DOOBAGE

When science-types at the University of New Haven in Connecticut found occasion to stare at some marijuana under a microscope, they discovered an unsettling amount of mold that couldn't be seen by the naked eye. Delving further, they discovered a whole laundry list of filthiness hiding unseen in cannabis—things like salmonella, E. coli, and random insect parts. So, we're not saying you should wash off your weed before every use like store-bought vegetables or anything but...hmm. Actually, maybe you should consider that.

53 A SPLIFF A DAY
KEEPS THE TUMORS AWAY?

Two of the main components of cannabis, tetrahydrocannabinol and cannabidiol, appear to have been successful in shrinking brain tumors, according to a recent study. So, hopefully we can add that to the list of ways marijuana fiddles with our brains, in addition to pain relief, appetite increase, and hilarious paranoia.

54 BRONCO
LOCO

Some wild animals seem to enjoy getting stoned just as much as humans. And though none as yet have been recorded rolling their own blunts, they do take advantage of the vegetation around them that offers mind-altering experiences. One example is horses' fondness for "locoweed," an addictive grass that is actually poisonous over time. It's basically a sort of trippy nicotine for horses.

55 UCLA FOR THE WIN

With findings that "were against our expectations," researchers at the University of California, Los Angeles, determined that pot smoking, whether done periodically or fiendishly, does not lead to lung cancer. Despite believing that they would come to some very different conclusions, one of the physicians involved (who had been studying marijuana for thirty years) revealed that, "What we found instead was no association at all, and even a suggestion of some protective effect."

56 POT POISONING

It's hard to die from marijuana poisoning, but apparently it is possible. It was reported that a British man, after smoking six joints a day for eleven years, succumbed to "cannabis toxicity." The attending doctor went on to note that "this type of death is extremely rare." And while he admitted that he had never seen a similar case in his entire career, "it corrects the argument that cannabis cannot kill anybody."

57 BAD DOGGY

The maned wolf is a freakish-looking canine from South America that looks like a coyote on stilts. Its appearance isn't the strangest thing about this creature, however. That would be reserved for the fact that its pee smells exactly like marijuana, so much so that it's not uncommon for police to be called to zoos to track down the pot smokers, when it's actually just the pungent squirts that came out of a wolf.

58 HAPPY SMOKE

It's been suggested in the past that marijuana use can be linked to depression and anxiety-related disorders. But a recent study in the journal *JAMA Psychiatry* that surveyed 35,000 American adults seems to have come to the opposite conclusion—that there is no link whatsoever between smoking weed and either of the aforementioned mental conditions.

59 BOOZE OVER BUDS

A risk assessment conducted by an international team of researchers in 2015 concluded that the risks inherent in marijuana consumption have been "overestimated," while the detrimental effects of drinking alcohol have been "underestimated." Their findings led them to announce that governments should place a greater priority on alcohol and tobacco management, and "a strict legal regulatory approach [for cannabis] rather than the current prohibition approach." And apparently the leaders in Ottawa actually listened.

60 WHY "MARIJUANA"?

The origin of the word "marijuana" comes from a mangling of the Spanish words *mariguana* or *marihuana*, both terms for the plant species Cannabis sativa. Or, if you would rather save lots of time and letters, you could just go with the English word, "hemp." Or one of the thousands of slang words in existence. Just don't say "wacky tobacky" anymore. It's embarrassing.

61 SMOKE THE WORM

Anecdotal reports abound of a menace to marijuana plants called "THC worms." Whether these creatures are real or the product of inebriated imaginations is open to debate, but they're often described as neon-orange colored, and plump with THC, prompting a brave few to consider eating them like tequila grubs. This isn't recommended, since if they are a real thing, they're most likely a bug called corn earworms, and are about as delicious as they sound.

PEW PEW
COUGH
PEW PEW

Marijuana and video games have always had a special relationship, but few would argue that smoking weed actually makes you more skilled at playing. Except that it actually might. Professional gaming circuits have reportedly had to place a strict ban on pre-competition cannabis consumption because it may be giving players an unfair advantage. A tournament director named Alex Walker revealed in an interview, "I've seen a number of players at national tournaments who came in 'baked' purely so they could play better."

AGING
RADICALLY

According to research from a Dutch organization called the Groningen Mental Enhancement Department, regular pot smoking may actually improve short-term memory retention—as long as you're a gamer too. They found that Alzheimer's patients who played video games and smoked pot, as opposed to those who merely played games, had 43 percent better memory retention. Maybe Alex Walker was on to something...

64 NOW DON'T GO START SMOKING SAILS

The word "canvas" seems like a pretty innocuous word, but its origin is directly related to marijuana. According to Dictionary.com, it likely comes from the Anglo-French word *canevas*, which traces its roots back to the Vulgar Latin adjective *cannabāceus* (literally translated as "made of hemp").

65 A TOXIC LUNGFUL

With all the talk about how beneficial marijuana can be, you shouldn't blind yourself to the fact that putting smoke of whatever variety into your lungs can be hazardous. A recent study revealed that, in some ways, pot smoking can put even more toxic stuff inside you than cigarettes. Since cannabis smoke is held inside the lungs longer, it just adds to the reality that the average toot contains twenty times more ammonia than a cigarette puff, five times more hydrogen cyanide, and five times the concentration of circulatory/immune system–ravaging nitrogen oxides. You can argue with the results all you want, but know this: their finding should be pretty accurate, since they used weed-smoking robots.

66 SOCIAL WEEDIA

The app known as High There! is designed to let weed enthusiasts connect with one another and has been described as the stoner version of Tinder. After punching in vitals like your mood, whether you prefer smoking or eating your cannabis, and your "energy preference," hopefully you'll get a match and be given the opportunity to meet a new friend and see where it takes you. Which hopefully isn't the trunk of a car on the way to a deserted quarry.

67 THE CANARY IN THE POT MINE

My Canary is an app created by a United States advocacy group called the National Organization for the Reform of Marijuana Laws (better known as NORML) that lets you figure out just how stoned you are. It guides you in conducting a series of tests on yourself in the areas of coordination, reflexes, balance, and reasoning, and could be the difference between life and death if you were flirting with the idea of operating a forklift in traffic right after smoking a joint.

68 A CHRONIC LIMP

A bit of a downer here, so to speak. Just to prove that moderation is key when it comes to most fun things, heavy pot smoking can result in some bad news in the bedroom. But first the good news: studies have shown that casual users of marijuana may experience little to no deleterious effects to their sexual performance, and weed may in fact improve your love life due to the way it reduces inhibitions and stimulates desire. However, smoking pot daily makes men three times as likely to experience erectile dysfunction than those who don't partake at all.

69 CHRONIC KINGPIN ON THE GO

If video games tend to be a little violent for your tastes and you're looking for something a bit more mellow, there's always Hemp Inc. This marijuana empire simulation game lets you grow the product and then sell it, while you hobnob with celebrities like Snoop Dogg, Wiz Khalifa, and Miley Cyrus. Not sure how much of a selling point that is, but there you go.

70 CHRONIC WEIGHT LOSS

A study of upwards of 5,000 people published in *The American Journal of Medicine* claims that people who smoke weed on a regular basis have thinner waistlines. Upon hearing about the study, Taco Bell immediately began researching a healthier menu.

71 WOMEN BAKE HARDER?

Recent research has shown that estrogen increases one's sensitivity to the effects of marijuana, meaning females get higher than males—at least that's true for the rats they performed the study on. However, the reaction known as "the munchies" seemed to be more prevalent in the males. We can only assume the scientists took into account the many variables involved, such as the differing levels of cheesiness between Nacho and Cool Ranch Doritos.

72 WEED REALLY DOES
BOOST CREATIVITY

Everyone has a few stoner friends who insist they just can't get the creative juices flowing without a little bud. Well, as it turns out, there might actually be something to their claims. A group of scientists studied the link between marijuana and creativity and postulated that ingesting cannabis causes temporary symptoms resembling psychosis. As a result, the user is better able to create links between seemingly unrelated concepts, a defining characteristic of creativity.

73 GROWING STRONGER
EVERY DAY

Have you ever heard older folks remark on how much stronger today's pot is than the wacky weed of their youth? Well, they're absolutely right. At least according to a study by the United States Drug Enforcement Administration, which found that the THC content in the average joint has about tripled since the mid-1990s.

74 WEED KEEPS
YOUR BRAIN HEALTHY

In a 2008 study, Ohio State University researchers found a link between properties in red wine (polyphenols) and properties in pot (THC) that can work to keep your brain healthy and nimble as you age. While the experts in the study wouldn't go so far as to endorse marijuana to help ward off such diseases as Alzheimer's, they said that the psychoactive agent in cannabis can reduce inflammation in the brain and perhaps even stimulate growth of brain cells.

75 CYBER
CANNABIS

It's no secret that some people abuse the medical marijuana system by claiming to have an illness when they don't. So a biotech company called PotBotics decided to eliminate the chicanery by creating the BrainBot, which enables physicians to use electroencephalography (EEG) to calculate exactly how an individual's brain might benefit from the use of cannabis. Other products that the company has developed include PotBot, an app that acts as a virtual "budtender," recommending the right strains and consumption methods for a person's specific medical ailments, and a program called NanoPot, which looks at the DNA of marijuana seeds for growers wishing to optimize their growth potential. You can basically think of the company's founder, David Goldstein, as the Bill Gates of people who enjoy Pink Floyd laser light shows.

76 **BAKE-BOT**
2000

A company called Automated Hydroponics Solutions has created a robot to assist with the growing of marijuana plants. The GroPro Hydroponics Supercharger acts as an environmental overseer for crops, and is described as a "state-of-the-art environmental robot that will manage your hydroponics system for optimal growth." Hopefully working in close proximity to so much cannabis will temper any overwhelming desires to destroy mankind.

77 THE FULL PACKAGE
...OR BAGGIE, IF YOU WILL

Leafly is one of the oldest and most highly respected marijuana-related apps around. Self-described as "the world's cannabis information resource," it provides just about all the information a weed enthusiast could ever ask for, such as retail locations, pot news and reviews, and special deals. Just imagine how successful they'd be if the name of their product didn't sound like something Angelina Jolie might name one of her adopted orphans.

78 WEED WEAKENS
THE IMMUNE SYSTEM

Although some people argue that grass should be legalized as a way of treating the symptoms of AIDS, cancer, and other diseases, a lot of medical folks suggest that when smoked in excess, weed can be harmful to people with compromised immune systems. Regularly using pot weakens your body's natural defense systems, including macrophages (cells that attack and kill invading viruses) and T-cells. If that's the case—and there's a lot of research to suggest that it is—smoking grass to feel better after chemotherapy is probably at least as damaging to your body as the chemicals themselves.

79 MARIJUANA SIZZLES
BRAIN CELLS

Researchers have found that THC suppresses the information-processing system of the hippocampus, the part of the brain that's involved in learning, memory, and mixing sensory experiences with emotions and motivations. So, if smoking marijuana feels like it's making you stupider...well, that's pretty much what it's doing.

80 SMOKING + PREGNANCY = NO GO

Most women know they shouldn't smoke cigarettes or drink alcohol while pregnant. But there's a myth out there that somehow this doesn't apply to marijuana. However, smoking pot during pregnancy can affect your baby in various ways, all of them bad. Studies have shown that children whose mothers smoked weed during pregnancy have trouble focusing and problem-solving. One study found such children were at greater risk for leukemia.

81 IF YOU STUDIED STONED, YOU CAN TAKE THE TEST STONED

Thanks to a phenomenon known as "state-dependent" learning, it's not a good idea to study for a test or prepare for a presentation while under the influence of marijuana, unless you also intend to take your test or give your presentation while you're stoned. Studies have shown that subjects performed better on memory recall tasks if they were high while memorizing *and* when asked to recall the information.

THREE

WEED AND
THE LAW

Despite it now being legal, for most of its history weed has been very much illegal. However, that hasn't stopped people from smoking it. This has led to some wacky mishaps, interesting court cases, and some really, really dumb criminals. Someday, perhaps, we'll look back on cannabis-related crimes like the ones on the next few pages and laugh. Or cry. Or maybe a weird combination of the two because we're just so high.

82 ODOR IN THE COURT

A few years ago a Toronto defense attorney was accused of representing his client a little *too* vigorously: by smuggling marijuana into jail for him. A guard testified that after the lawyer's visit, they found fifty-eight grams of weed wrapped in cellophane, some rolled up joints, and lidocaine in the inmate's underwear. The attorney was found innocent, however, after the judge declared the guards to be "unreliable historians" who claimed they smelled pot on the lawyer from the start but also "violated protocol" during their search. Whether the lawyer did it or not, at the very least the incident should do wonders for his practice.

83 I AM THE MOOSE

In 2014, when a moose in Vermont wandered into a commercial parking lot, police were summoned to chase the interloping beast back into the woods. The case then took an entirely different turn as the cops tried coaxing the moose toward its natural habitat. It led them to a shed that smelled rather suspicious, which contained a stockpile of more than thirty illegally grown marijuana plants. Presumably satisfied with a job well done, the moose then probably made its way back to its secret Moose Cave to prepare for another day of fighting crime.

84 GANJA GOONS

The National Hockey League is a little different from other professional sports organizations in that it's pretty lax when it comes to punishing players for smoking weed. While soccer and basketball players can get suspended and even jeopardize their entire careers by getting photographed hitting a bong, hockey players can smoke freely without the risk of any punishment whatsoever. Perhaps the league just feels that it's the least it can do, after having caused so many young men to give up their teeth in battle.

85 HIGH FIVE

When pro football players run afoul of the National Football League by getting caught smoking weed, they can always run off to Canada. The Canadian Football League has served as a second chance for many toke-happy players, since while the league does test for and punish those who use performance-enhancing drugs, it has no such policy for marijuana. Which makes a certain sense, since every team in the league plays on AstroTurf instead of natural grass.

86 MAYBE THEY JUST FOUND A REALLY BAD ZOO?

When the authorities raided a couple of pot farms in Vancouver, they found the site guarded by some rather unexpected security guards. The operators had apparently lured over a dozen semi-tame bears into the area to protect the property, in addition to several raccoons and pigs. Whether they were all suffering from glaucoma was not mentioned in the report.

87 RIDING DIRTY

The late Rob Ford, former mayor of Toronto, may have been most infamous for his crackpipe proclivities, but cocaine wasn't the only intoxicant he dabbled in. Back in 1999, he was picked up on a DUI in Miami after a romantic (and wine-soaked) Valentine's Day dinner with his wife. During the arrest, he was also charged with possession of marijuana, but somehow beat the charge on that one. Years later, when a reporter asked him about that night, he responded, "I completely forgot until you mentioned it right now. You think I'm BSing you, but I'm not. It completely, totally slipped my mind."

88 HERBAL HYPOCRISY

With marijuana still being illegal in 2013, Toronto became inundated with herbal substitutes, which most residents assumed were perfectly in accordance with the law. Authorities begged to differ, and took special offense at a colorfully packaged product called "the Izms," which they believed was an attempt to attract children. And so the police proceeded to conduct raids on downtown Izms purveyors with the goal of ridding their fair city of the offending herbs. In response, the company behind the product issued just one public statement on its *Facebook* page: "Our mayor smokes crack yet police harass the izms. Wtf? A little backwards no?"

89 WOULD YOU LIKE BUDS WITH THAT?

A Tim Hortons franchise in Halifax was discovered to be giving certain customers a little something extra with their drive-thru orders. The manager became suspicious when two of his young employees were serving customers who requested Timbits in "15-packs" along with a cup of coffee, because there was no such thing as a 15-pack and no free coffee giveaway. It turned out that the customers were merely using a code to let the workers know they were in the mood less for pastry, and more for pot hidden in empty coffee cups.

YOU CAN'T HAVE
JUST ONE

Border agents at the Wild Horse border crossing in Alberta apprehended a man who was attempting to smuggle marijuana in a very clever way—by stashing several grams into a tube of potato chips modified with a false bottom. While it didn't effectively conceal the weed, it did solve the problem of keeping his weed and munchies in a handy, centralized location.

91 CAN YOU DIG IT?

Three Canadian men were arrested on drug charges in 2005 after border authorities were tipped off to the very first known smuggling tunnel dug underneath the Canada-US border. United States officials discovered the three men sneaking out of their tunnel on the US side after nightfall. Reports unfortunately don't mention whether or not the men were dressed in gopher costumes and claimed immunity as an endangered species.

92 YOU SHOULD ALWAYS HAVE A BACKUP

A Canadian man was plucked out of the St. Clair River along the Canada-US border after United States Air Force observer planes spotted him swimming suspiciously across in full SCUBA gear. US Border Patrol agents discovered that the man had been towing a sealed cylinder filled with eight pounds of weed behind him under the water. We'll assume the authorities were skeptical if his excuse was that he thought he was dragging a spare air tank.

93 SLIPPERY SLOPE

When mountain resorts in the Calgary area began experiencing skiers sneaking a toke on the chairlifts and gondolas, the Mounties swooped in, patrolling the slopes on skis and snowboards. Some even went undercover to catch vacationers who ducked behind a tree or into a smoke shack for a one-hitter. Some begrudgingly applauded their efforts when incidents of theft and other lawlessness went down, as one visitor remarked: "It makes sense. It sucks, but it makes sense." But others weren't quite so enthusiastic about the lack of privacy, saying, "I feel like the chairlift is my time to smoke reefer."

94 YOU DON'T SEE KINGPINS NAMED ABRAHAM ANYMORE

Canada has to deal with its fair share of illegal transporters, and oddly enough some of the major players in that game are...Mennonites. You know, the folks with the horses and buggies that are just slightly less intense than the Amish? There's even a Mennonite crime family, started by a man named Abraham Harms, who, after being charged with smuggling marijuana into Ontario, fled the country to conduct his sneaky business down in Mexico.

95 INTERNATIONAL COOPERATION

The Akwesasne Indian Reserve is unique in that it's the only First Nations reserve that sits directly on the border between the United States and Canada. This situation also presents a unique opportunity for smugglers, and, beginning in 1999, a drug operation took full advantage of the easy border crossings, raking in $30 million a year. At least half of the members of the ring were part of the Saint Regis Mohawk Tribe that lives on the reserve. When the operation was finally taken down, it was described as "by far the biggest marijuana ring the [US Drug Enforcement Agency] has ever busted in Upstate New York."

96 YOU CAN PICK SOME UP ON YOUR WAY TO BEST BUY

Law enforcement officials once stumbled upon more than 200 marijuana plants growing in a makeshift greenhouse inside a mall in Florida. The small room came complete with a surveillance system, air conditioning, and an elaborate hydroponic growing system, and housed plants ranging from three to six feet tall. Because the plants could be harvested several times a year, police estimated their value to be several million dollars.

97 I...I DON'T THINK THAT'S TRUE

A Canadian woman was pulled over in the United States after police noticed her driving on the wrong side of the road. After the cops found a stash of marijuana (and meth, which probably explains the next part) inside her vehicle, her excuse for her behavior was that "Canadians drive on the left side of the road."

98 AN UNPLEASANT EXPERIENCE

Legendary guitarist Jimi Hendrix was no stranger to Canada, but may have spent a little more time there than he would have liked in 1969 when Mounties detained him at what was then called the Toronto International Airport. Found to be carrying hashish and other drugs, as well as paraphernalia, in his luggage, he would find himself facing charges in court. Luckily, his lawyer was able to make the case that all that stuff was just a gift given to Hendrix by a fan and that he had no clue that he was actually carrying illegal drugs. And even better, the legal record now includes a case that sounds like an epic rock battle: *Queen vs. James Marshall Hendrix.*

99 TASTIES, NOT TICKETS

After it was announced that the state of Washington planned to legalize marijuana, police in Seattle took a more welcoming approach than normal at the next year's weed-celebrating festival Hempfest: they passed out Doritos. Instead of hand-cuffs and citations, police dis-tributed an estimated one thousand bags of chips, each affixed with a sticker explain-ing the specifics of the state's new recreational marijuana law.

100 YEAH, GOOD LUCK WITH THAT

A man in California is suing his local law enforcement for lost profit over the destruction of the ninety-three marijuana plants that were taken from his house when he was arrested under charges of marijuana sales. Kirk David Stewart claimed the plants should have been returned to him when the case was dismissed. Because the sheriff's department destroyed the plants, Stewart claimed he should get the fair market value for the plants, which would have totaled several hundred thousand US dollars.

101 WEED GOGGLES

Don't think that merely because you have your pot crop hidden in a corn field you're good to go. Police in Zurich, Switzerland, got a lucky break when Googling the address of two farmers they were investigating as part of a larger drug operation. When the Google Earth satellite map came up, the officers clearly spotted the two-acre patch of weed that was being grown inside of a corn field. The find helped in the investigation of the larger drug operation that led to sixteen arrests and the seizure of 1.2 tons of marijuana.

102 SELLING WEED ON CRAIGSLIST—BAD IDEA

Sometimes in life you should make the extra effort instead of taking the easy way out. Steven Zahorsky couldn't be bothered to actively try to sell his weed and instead made a posting on *Craigslist* for the product. His post worked—he received a response from a man looking to buy three-quarters of an ounce of weed. Unfortunately, that man was a police officer. The officer said he was part of a painting crew that was looking to buy some weed. They arranged to meet at a highway rest stop, where they made the exchange and the officer promptly arrested Zahorsky.

103 YOU CAN'T MAKE IT MUCH EASIER ON THE POLICE

A man in Washington State was smart in looking to hide his stash before he appeared in court. Unfortunately, his hiding spot was not ideal—under a bush outside the sheriff detectives' window. The detectives saw Eugenio Anthony Colon hide the container in the bush and confronted the man, who was in the courthouse for an unrelated matter, while he awaited his court appearance. Colon told the detectives that he didn't realize they were there or could see him. With a defense like that, who needs lawyers?

104 CANDIDATES FOR THE DUMBEST CRIMINAL AWARD

What do weed aficionados Michael Omelchunk, Stephen Knight, and Cory Oxtoby have in common? They all called the police to report that their weed had been stolen. Omelchunk's stash was stolen from him in his apartment by two armed men. The police found more weed that wasn't stolen and arrested him. Knight also had thieves break in, but he was hogtied with Christmas lights before they stole his stuff. Police also found more drugs in his place and arrested him. And Oxtoby was robbed at gunpoint while he was trying to make a sale in a Walmart parking lot. He was also arrested when he called police to report the theft. Make sure you never challenge these clowns for the Dumbest Criminal Award.

105 IT REALLY ISN'T EASY BEING GREEN

A man from the United States claimed that the large amount of pot that police officers found in his car was not for smoking but for compost. The officers didn't buy his load of...compost, and arrested him. He was charged with processing marijuana with intent to distribute.

106 DO YOU HAVE
CHANGE FOR AN OUNCE?

No matter how badly you have the munchies, never try paying for your late-night feast with weed. Shawn Pannullo learned this seemingly simple lesson the hard way when he tried to barter food for weed in a US McDonald's. Just after midnight one night, Pannullo ordered through the drive-thru, but left when the cashier refused to take the trade. She called the police and gave them the description of Pannullo's car. This led to his arrest a short time later and a charge of marijuana possession. And to top it all off, he went to jail hungry.

107 HEMP
HEAVEN

If you're going to grow pot, you shouldn't plant it at a nunnery—religious karma is terrible to deal with. In Athens, Greece, two men approached some elderly nuns and offered to help with their garden. Instead of planting tulips and roses, however, they planted thirty cannabis plants. Police received a tip about the garden and found the plants. The nuns, who thought the weed was merely "large decorative plants," were not arrested.

108 YOU SHOULD BE WORRIED YOUR KIDS ARE MESSED UP WHEN...

Three surprisingly dedicated teens in Texas, looking for something to smoke out of, decided it would be a good idea to dig up a grave, steal a skull, and turn it into a bong. According to the teens, they spent two days digging up the grave of an eleven-year-old boy who died in 1921, and they used a gardening tool to remove the boy's skull from his skeleton. One of the boys told the police about the grave robbery when he was being investigated for a car robbery. The boys were charged with abuse of a corpse and a vehicle break-in.

109 STONY SYNONYMS

If you think you know a lot of slang words for marijuana, chances are you don't even know a portion of what the US government has gathered over the years. They have a list of more than five hundred synonyms for "reefer" (there's one!) in their official database, which include some obscure gems like "Boo Boo Bama," "Dinkie Dow," and "Assassin of Youth."

110 THAT'S NO YULE LOG

After a fifty-year-old woman in San Bernardo, Chile, bragged to her neighbors that she had the "best Christmas tree in the world," authorities disagreed when they discovered it was actually a huge marijuana plant. As festive as her presentation was, with presents surrounding it, it didn't prevent the police from taking her into custody. After the raid on the woman's home, one of her neighbors came to a realization and remarked, "Thinking about it, she didn't invite me in to see her tree."

111 LET'S KEEP IT
ALL-NATURAL, FOLKS

Rogue illegal pot growers are not just a danger to the land and the surrounding flora—they also pose a grave threat to the local fauna. In California, endangered species are being killed from the rodent poisons being spread around by pot farmers. The Pacific fisher, a weasel-like animal, has been particularly affected, with 85 percent of tested fishers showing exposure to the poisons.

"THIS STUFF IS THE BOMB! OOPS..."

112

Now that Oregon has legalized recreational marijuana, you can actually transport less than an ounce of weed on an airplane as long as the flight begins and ends within the confines of the state. According to a spokesperson from the US Transportation Security Administration (TSA), their job is to "detect threats to aviation security," and not hassle adults who are abiding by the state's laws. Since weed is now legal up here, do you think we can do this too?

HASSLE-FREE EUROPE

113

If you thought Amsterdam was the best place in Europe to get stoned without the pesky side effects of lengthy jail sentences, you'd be wrong. The fact is that selling marijuana is still illegal there. Police just don't really get involved with the pot shops there and basically let them slide. The loosest drug laws are actually in Portugal, which decided in 2001 to become the first European nation to completely decriminalize the personal possession of everything from weed to heroin. Their rationale was simple: since sending people to jail costs so much and the fear of being sent there forces addicts into hiding, why not save a few bucks and offer treatment instead of prison terms?

114 JUST SAY NO (AT LEAST IN SINGAPORE)

East Asia in general is a very, very bad place to get caught dealing drugs, but Singapore might be the most nightmarish. If they find you carrying more than five hundred grams of marijuana and decide you're a trafficker, you'll be facing mandatory execution. And no, it won't be by the "we're going to make you smoke the whole thing" method.

115 THAT'S SOME TOP-SHELF WEED

It happens to the best of us. You pull someone over and steal their weed, bake it into brownies that you eat with your wife, freak out and think you're dead, and call 911. Or maybe not all of us, but it did happen to a former American police officer named Edward Sanchez. Sanchez and his wife ate the stolen pot-filled brownies and proceeded to have such a bad trip that they thought the pot might have been laced with something. "I think we're dying. I think we're dead. I really do," Sanchez told the dispatcher during his five-minute-long call. "Time is going by really, really, really, really slow." Sanchez resigned from his post and was not prosecuted.

NORTH KOREA ISN'T
QUITE AS GROOVY
AS THE RUMORS SUGGEST

116

There's a persistent claim floating around the Internet that weed is totally legal over there in Kim Jong-un's Democratic People's Republic of Korea (more commonly known as North Korea) and that it's some sort of pot-smoker's paradise. The reality is that smoking marijuana is most certainly frowned upon in North Korea, in the sense that there's a very good chance they'll shoot you in the face for possessing it. And knowing them, that could very well be one of the better case scenarios.

FROM REPORTER
TO ACTIVIST

117

Charlo Greene, the Alaska TV reporter who famously quit her job on the air while reporting on her own marijuana company, followed that well-thought-out life choice by announcing she would become a full-time cannabis activist. Her exploits were celebrated by *High Times* with a Courage in Media award and her inclusion on *Elle* magazine's list of "13 Most Potent Women in the Pot Industry."

118 AT LEAST HE HAD GOOD SNACKS TO HELP HIM THROUGH

There's no shame in not being able to handle psychotropic drugs—you should just be aware of your limits. Don't be like the unfortunate American man who called 911 in a panic and told the dispatcher he was "too high." According to CBS News, when police responded, they found the poor guy in a fetal position, "surrounded by a plethora of Doritos, Pepperidge Farm Goldfish, and Chips Ahoy cookies," complaining that he couldn't feel his hands. Although they found him to be illegally in possession of a small amount of pot, authorities initially refrained from seeking charges, possibly out of pity.

119 SO THAT'S WHAT BUNSEN BURNERS ARE FOR

Everyone remembers a "cool" teacher from back in high school. You know, the one who wore his tie just a little bit loose, was always ready with a joke, and let the students smoke weed with abandon during shop class. Wait a minute...Being that lenient is probably somewhat ill-advised, as Domonic Leuzzi, a teacher in Virginia (who actually did that) would probably tell you. He is no longer employed by the school system and was arrested for "contributing to the delinquency of a minor."

120 BOB MARLEY CAN FINALLY REST PEACEFULLY

As famous as Jamaica is for Rastafarians and ganja-loving reggae musicians, smoking marijuana was illegal there until 2015, when the government finally bowed to all the dreadlocked pressure and decriminalized possession (at least for small amounts). But don't get any bright ideas about cross-border trafficking, unless you want your vacation to turn from two weeks into twenty-five-to-life.

121 "DRUG DEALER" IS GREAT ON A RESUME

After serving ten years in prison for smuggling an estimated seventy-five tons of marijuana into the United States, Brian O'Dea took out a classified ad in the *National Post* looking for legitimate work. He cited his experience running a $100 million drug business as his primary qualification, and received nearly six hundred job offers.

 122 MAYBE IT HELPS
PREVENT MEMORY LOSS?

Here's a good reason to always purchase your marijuana from a reputable source. Police in Pennsylvania arrested a man who had a habit of smoking "wet marijuana"—pot soaked in formaldehyde. But that's not even close to the worst part of the story. The formaldehyde the man dipped his pot into was in a laboratory jar containing a human brain. Police believe the brain was a stolen teaching specimen, and a spokesman said they were hoping to return it to its "rightful owner." Sadly, chances are he or she may be deceased.

 123 CURIOUSER AND
CURIOUSER!

In the spring of 2015, police in Cheshire, England (the childhood home of *Alice in Wonderland* author Lewis Carroll), raided a country mansion and discovered a pot farm worth £750,000. A monstrous, hookah-sucking caterpillar presumably fled the area beforehand after being tipped off by a spastic rabbit and a peculiar individual wearing a huge, ridiculous hat.

124 IS THERE A CHIHUAHUA ON COCAINE?

Singapore is one of the riskier places in the world to light up, what with its harsh no-tolerance laws. And to drive that point home, the country's Central Narcotics Bureau has come up with a campaign that's sure to make visitors and locals alike say nope to dope and ugh to drugs—with posters featuring hip but addled cartoon characters like a heroin-addicted bear, an "ice"-gobbling chicken, and Nash the cannabis cat.

125 GETTING HIGH IS A RELIGIOUS SACRAMENT

Marijuana use may be illegal in Italy, but that law does not apply to everyone. Members of the Rastafari religion are permitted to carry small amounts of marijuana for personal use, as it is considered a sacrament. The amount a Rastafarian can carry for "personal use" is relatively vague; however, it's been deemed that an amount equivalent to approximately seventy joints is permissible.

 126 CONFOUNDING THE CARTELS

The US Border Patrol has been waging a losing battle against the flow of illegal drugs that are constantly being smuggled in by the Mexican drug cartels. But the recent legalization of marijuana in certain states seems to be having a tangible effect. The agency has reported that they're finally seeing less weed coming across, and in 2014 the Mexican Army also reported that marijuana seizures were down 32 percent from the previous year.

 127 EL CHAPO MEETS MACGYVER

Although legal weed is wreaking havoc on the Mexican cartels' smuggling operations, that doesn't mean they've stopped sneaking it over by any means at their disposal. Tunnels and packages hidden in car tires are just the tip of the iceberg in terms of their criminal ingenuity. Other methods of getting their product from point A to point B have included catapults, drones, submarines, hollowed-out fake carrots, and even stuffing large amounts of weed inside dead, frozen sharks.

128 INSANE IN THE MEMBRANE

Here's a good argument for staying natural as opposed to dabbling in synthetic fakery. In the summer of 2016, a number of New York City residents partook in the man-made pot doppelgänger called K2, which is made by spraying various chemicals on plants that most certainly are not marijuana. It had a much stronger effect than expected, leaving dozens of people stumbling through the streets with blank stares. One witness said, "it looked like a scene out of a zombie movie."

 LEADING THE WORLD

In 2013, Uruguay was the first country to fully legalize the sale and use of recreational marijuana. The new law limits cannabis enthusiasts to 1.4 ounces per month, and insists the drug be purchased from licensed pharmacies by customers eighteen or older. The law also entitles citizens to grow up to six marijuana plants in their home.

 CRIME-FIGHTING CANNABIS

A recent British study published in the renowned scientific journal *PLOS ONE* showed that marijuana use does not lead to crime. Or at least legalized weed doesn't. The research revealed that when cannabis was decriminalized in an area of London, crime rates either remained exactly the same or even decreased. It also appeared to help the police, as they were free to focus their energies elsewhere rather than busting random teenagers with joints in their pockets.

131 GANJA FROM HEAVEN

Several years ago, the peace and quiet of a family in the southwestern United States was rudely interrupted when a nearly thirty-pound package of marijuana fell out of a clear blue sky, crashed through their carport, and crushed their dog crate. Thankfully, the crate was unoccupied at the time. How could such a thing happen? The most likely explanation is that they live just a few miles from the US–Mexico border and in the likely path of a smuggling operation. Either that or the dog needs to find a dealer who's a bit more discreet with his deliveries.

132 GETTING IN TOUCH WITH YOUR LIZARD BRAIN

A man in the US thought it would be funny to put a video on YouTube of himself getting high with his pet chameleon and blowing the smoke in the lizard's face. A lot of other people apparently found it hilarious as well, as the video went viral. But unfortunately the clip became popular enough to catch the attention of local authorities, who charged the man with animal abuse. A judge took pity, however, and acquitted him of all charges, deeming his behavior "immature but not criminal." Oh, the man's name? Bruce Blunt.

 133 EVERY. SINGLE. ONE.

According to the US Drug Enforcement Agency, cannabis is being grown (legally or otherwise) in every single state in the union, as well as the US Virgin Islands and Puerto Rico.

 134 THE TWO FACES OF MICKEY

A recent ordinance change may make it so that getting caught with pot at Disney World won't result in an arrest (but presumably will still earn a stern finger-wagging from Goofy). Well, depending which part of the park you're in at the time. See, the Disney property spans two Florida counties, and if you're caught on one side of the county line with a small amount of weed in your pocket, you might just get a fine. But if you're on the other side, they'll still lock you up while you sputter and curse like Donald Duck.

135 SILVER LINING: AT LEAST HE DOESN'T HAVE TO PAY RENT ANYMORE

Seventy-six-year-old Lee Carroll Brooker was sentenced to life in prison in Alabama recently, thanks to the "excessive and unjustified" (according to the chief justice of the state's Supreme Court) legal system of the state. His crime? Getting caught with a number of marijuana plants that were reportedly for his own use, as treatment for his chronic pain. The reason the judgment was so harsh was that Brooker had been convicted of a felony more than thirty years prior.

136 DOOBIE-FREE DUBAI

If you're traveling to Dubai, take a break from your favorite pastime until your visit is concluded. Just ask Keith Brown, a British traveler who was arrested and sentenced to four years in prison after airport customs officials discovered a speck of weed, "smaller than a grain of sugar," stuck to the underside of his shoe.

137 THAT WATCHDOG APPEARS TO BE A REPTILE

We know that illicit marijuana farmers have been known to employ wild bears, raccoons, and hogs as their version of junkyard dogs, but it gets crazier: a caiman, a reptile similar to an alligator, was found guarding a stash in a house in Northern California.

138 A MONSTROUS ESCAPE

Game wardens in Texas discovered a huge grow operation that contained 6,550 individual plants. Their subsequent hunt for the operators was stymied, however, when their search was thrown off course by people claiming to be hunting for Bigfoot. That was either a lucky break for the perpetrators or one of the most ingenious escape strategies ever.

139 BAMBI'S TEENAGE YEARS

The cover of an illegal Italian marijuana-growing operation was blown when police started noticing that the deer in the area were acting "unusually frisky." The locals had also been observing the animals acting strangely and "making great leaps on the mountainside." According to reports, the culprits were all apprehended, but perhaps not for long since the deer had apparently eaten all the evidence.

140 GET READY FOR THE WEEDALYZER

US law enforcement recently debuted the first breath-alyzer able to detect the presence of marijuana. Not only can this technology tell when you've smoked pot, it can even determine when you've eaten food that contained it. So even if you sprinkle marijuana into your spicy taco while driving, no amount of salsa will hide your misdeeds.

141 SWEATY FINGERS TELL TALES

As if breathalyzers that can detect marijuana weren't ominous enough for the weed enthusiast, there's also a fingerprint scanner in the works that can tell from your sweat if there's any cannabis in your system. The scanner can even tell if you've recently shaken hands with someone who was high, so you might want to stick with fist bumps the next time you're surrounded by hippies.

142 FEISTY FARMERS

Authorities in Liberia recently turned their attention to marijuana farmers. The locals didn't take too kindly to these measures, setting up roadblocks and threatening the police with guns and whatever else was at hand. According to the executive director of Liberia's Drug Enforcement Agency, "People came with machetes and sticks and they started beating up the DEA men. These guys had to jump in the bush."

143 BUZZED DETECTORS

Drug-sniffing dogs may have some competition soon, as tests are being conducted to see whether bees, moths, or even cockroaches can do the job of detecting marijuana and other drugs hidden in luggage or wherever else. So far, the winner seems to be the bees, as their antennae make great "biosensors."

144 MIGHT AS WELL ORDER SOME PIZZA WHILE I HAVE YOU ON THE LINE

911 operators in Virginia received a call from a man in a "disoriented state." Their fears of a medical emergency began to diminish when he asked for someone to be sent to his house bringing rolling papers. Reports of the incident stated the rather obvious: that the police believed the man to be under the influence of marijuana.

145 NO HIGH-FLYING SOUVENIRS

Not everyone is on board with the state of Colorado becoming synonymous with all things marijuana-related in the United States. The Denver International Airport has banned the sale of all souvenirs that have a pot leaf logo on them, worrying that such items would tarnish the state's image. As if the Colorado Avalanche hadn't accomplished that already.

146 I'M SO WASTED

US stoner and country music singer Willie Nelson once said, "Marijuana won't kill you unless you let a bale of it fall on you." Which is sort of what happened when a Brazilian drug smuggler attempted to transport 1,100 pounds of weed in the back seat of his car. After being chased by police, the crook lost control of the vehicle and crashed head-on into a tree, which resulted in said bale of marijuana squashing him like a bug.

147 BUMPER CROP

Unfortunately for the citizens of central California, the area is one of the most popular places in America for Mexican cartels to set up illegal grow farms. In one month alone in 2009, American authorities confiscated $1 billion (yes, that's a "b") worth of pot in Operation Save Our Sierra, with eighty-two suspects arrested. Hopefully they didn't burn it all at once, or at least saved it for a special occasion.

148 WEED HELPS FIGHT THE COCAINE INDUSTRY

Colombia used to have an epidemic of homelessness and addiction surrounding a cocaine derivative known as *basuco*. The drug—a smokable extract similar to crack—is very addictive and often contains residue from solvents like kerosene, which is used to manufacture it. To solve the problem, officials in the capital city of Bogotá took a controversial approach: they provided addicts with marijuana as an alternative.

149 PLEASE DON'T LET THEM CHECK THE PIXIE STIX

A man was apprehended in a United States airport while trying to smuggle small amounts of marijuana hidden in the wrappers of an old-timey candy brand called Mary Jane. Not missing the irony, reports described his contraband as "artfully concealed."

150 GIVE EMPLOYMENT TO OUR CANINE PALS

In the dog world, there are certain Judases who shun the title of man's best friend and opt instead to pursue a career in professional snitching: they're trained to alert their handlers when they detect the presence of drugs such as marijuana. There's no current explanation for why these dogs have turned on their human companions, though it might have something to do with all the times humans got stoned and thought it would be funny to make them wear silly hats and sweaters.

151 THERE'S A FREAKING POT CANNON

Mexican police are no strangers to innovative methods for smuggling marijuana across the border into the United States. Case in point: they once stumbled upon an actual marijuana cannon. The device, which consisted of a long plastic pipe and a tank of compressed air, could fire packages of drugs as heavy as thirty pounds over the border.

152 A SQUIRRELLY ALIBI

In 2013, a man in Washington State was caught firing an arrow with a bag of pot attached to it over the walls of a county jail. When questioned, the thirty-six-year-old man said it was all a big mistake, and that he had actually been aiming at a squirrel. The squirrel could not be located to confirm whether this was indeed an interspecies drug deal gone wrong.

 THE FRIENDLY SKIES

Leading up to the legalization of marijuana in Colorado in 2014, there was some concern that tourists from states without legal weed would try to smuggle some back home. However, it turned out to be a lot of worry for nothing, as only ten people were stopped trying to smuggle and not a single citation for marijuana was issued at the airport through the first five months that it was legal. A spokesperson for the main airport for the state said, "To have contact with ten people out of millions passing through, it tells me most people are abiding by the rules and this is not a major issue."

 A STING FOILED BY A STING

When Russian police attempted to remove more than five hundred marijuana plants growing near the city of Kostroma, they were forced to abandon the operation after hundreds of angry bees began an all-out assault. When questioned, a local beekeeper insisted he had nothing to do with the marijuana growing on his land, but police suspect the bees might have been placed there deliberately to protect the crop.

155 HARSH PLAINS

The marijuana laws in South Dakota are pretty far from mellow. Not only is it illegal to possess weed in the state itself, it's also against the law to have traces of pot in your system, even if you imbibed it in another state entirely. Specifically, the law reads that it is illegal to ingest any "substance, except alcoholic beverages, for the purpose of becoming intoxicated." And where you happened to have ingested it makes no difference whatsoever.

156 SMOKED PORK

In the remote nation of Bhutan, the authorities are reportedly concerned about the increasing frequency of marijuana use among their young people. It's something they never had to really think about before, because despite the fact that cannabis grows wild all over the place and is readily available to anyone who wants some, nobody seems to have realized that it was a drug. Until recently, the plant had only been used to feed pigs.

157 COLD-BLOODED JUSTICE

An illegal marijuana-growing operation in Maryland was busted when an undercover operative infiltrated the facility and gathered all the necessary information to make the case. Who was this brave law enforcement hero protecting America from these drug lords? A turtle with a GPS monitor strapped to its shell.

158 THE MOTHER OF ALL STASHES

The biggest accumulation of stored marijuana (that we know of) is held under lock and key at the University of Mississippi. No, this isn't the location of Willie Nelson's Scrooge McDuck–style mountain of wallowing weed—it's the property of the US government. Apparently it's being kept for medical research, but that's not going on as effectively as it could be, since they have to get permission from the US Drug Enforcement Agency before they can do anything at all.

 159 TRUTH IN ADVERTISING

When a man was pulled over in Oregon for a traffic violation, the first thing officers noticed was that the man was wearing a toque with the word "WEED" emblazoned across the front. One of the next things they noticed was the fact that the man had $15,000 worth of marijuana stashed in the car.

 160 CAN'T BELIEVE YOUR EYES

Law enforcement in Georgia swooped in on a suspected marijuana growing facility. They came, ready for anything, with a helicopter, dogs, and a wide assortment of weaponry. Then things got stupid, as it soon became apparent that what the authorities saw from above wasn't cannabis at all, but a field full of okra.

161 WHY ARE THE POLICE DELIVERING MY ROOM SERVICE?

Some modern smoke detectors do more than just let you know the room's on fire. The AirGuard model can do that, sure, but it can also differentiate between different types of smoke, and let the hotel staff know when you've been dabbling in doobies in one of their suites. After detecting the organic compounds in marijuana, it won't necessarily start blaring an alarm, but might keep a log of your activities.

162 OPERATION OVERKILL

In Massachusetts, an eighty-one-year-old woman named Margaret Holcomb kept a single, solitary marijuana plant in order to help with her glaucoma, arthritis, and insomnia. This was apparently enough of a breach of the public peace to convince the Massachusetts State Police and Massachusetts National Guard to send numerous vehicles, along with a helicopter, to converge on her home in 2016. This was just part of a larger operation that saw forty-three homes raided that day, with some of the residents being guilty of an even greater crime than Ms. Holcomb's: having two plants.

163 A DUBIOUS PROPOSITION

In 2014, opponents of medical marijuana legalization in Florida took things to another level when they ran a TV spot linking cannabis use to date rape. In the ad, the makers claimed that if new medical marijuana legislation was passed, teenagers would have no problem getting their hands on pot. And then the query was posed: "Will the new face of date rape look like a [marijuana] cookie?" Presumably they nixed the ad that connected marijuana use to Hitler's rise to power.

164 MAYBE TRY THE BETTER BUSINESS BUREAU

An American woman called police to complain that she had been robbed. But sadly her quest for justice went unfulfilled when the cops heard her story—that she was disappointed in the quality of marijuana she had received from her dealer, and that said dealer had refused to return her money. To bolster her claim, she pulled out a sample from her bra to show the officers. Shockingly, she wound up getting arrested instead of the dealer.

165 PUNCHLINE POT
PURVEYORS

In the spring of 2017, taking its first steps into the cannabis industry, the state of Maryland granted only around fifteen licenses to legally sell marijuana, and competition to get them was fierce. To get to the front of the line, a little divine intervention certainly wouldn't hurt, so perhaps it makes sense that among the applicants in 2016 were a priest and a rabbi. Seriously, this isn't the start of a bad joke.

166 NO MORE TEARS
(OR JOB)

Just so you're aware, there are certain baby soaps and shampoos that can cause a false positive result in tests for marijuana. So weigh your options carefully—is having soft, lustrous hair (without the fear of openly weeping every time you get the stuff in your eyes) worth the price of being unemployed?

167 UFOS STOLE MY STASH!

Ingenious criminals in England have been using unmanned drones to pilfer pot from illegal grow sites after spotting them from the air with infrared cameras. The victims are easy targets, especially since they can't exactly go to the police and complain that sky robots stole their illegal weed.

168 FORESIGHT IS A GOOD THING

Weed paraphernalia can get pretty imaginative, but you might want to think twice about carrying around a grinder that looks exactly like a hand grenade. Especially should you happen to be getting ready to board a plane, for crying out loud. Which is what one traveler at an airport in the state of Washington did, sending airport security officials into a panic and causing several flights to be delayed.

FOUR

HOLLYWOOD HOPHEADS AND OTHER TOKERS

Many a celebrity has taken the edge off with a toke or two every now and again. Weed has long been integral to the creative process and whether they're in the arts (like Seth Rogen), tech (like Bill Gates), or any other industry, the high and powerful have often sparked up to try to inspire themselves. Drug-fueled dramas involving luminaries of the stage and screen have led to some of the greatest films, music, and innovations in our time. Kick back and light up knowing these great men and women smoke just like you.

169 THE CHONG SAGA BEGINS IN CALGARY

According to his biography, Tommy Chong first developed his love of herb in Canada: "I was introduced to pot by a Chinese jazz musician in Calgary, Canada, in 1957. He gave me a joint and a Lenny Bruce record and changed my life forever."

170 PRIME TIME PUFFING

The iconic Canadian sketch comedy show *SCTV* occasionally expanded beyond the McKenzie Brothers' love of beer and included marijuana references in their skits. In one of their most famous sketches, Rick Moranis, playing the part of revered newscaster David Brinkley, complains on national TV about a horrifying crisis: the declining quality of Lebanese hash.

 BABY, BABY, BABY

Canadian hero (or pariah) Justin Bieber was alleged in 2014 to have been smoking marijuana on a flight from his home country to the United States. Oh, his father was there as well—also smoking marijuana and refusing to stop when the pilot asked them to. It was an unbelievably insensitive move on the part of the pilot, if it should turn out that the Bieber family is genetically predisposed to cataracts.

 ALSO, TRY NOT TO SET YOURSELF ON FIRE

Early on in comedian Jim Carrey's career, when he first came to Los Angeles from Canada, he spent a lot of time at the Comedy Store where he was lucky enough to meet Richard Pryor. In addition to great advice, Pryor was generous with his weed—as well as a warning. According to Carrey, he said, "We were passing a joint one night, and he said, 'Careful with that: I don't remember forty years of my life.'"

173 THAT EXPLAINS
THE SHADES

Canadian actor Ryan Reynolds wasn't always a big-screen superhero. Back when he was a struggling nobody, his big chance came about through hard work, talent, and...the fact that Wesley Snipes loves weed. Thanks to Snipes' being constantly stoned on the set of *Blade: Trinity*, Reynolds was forced to improvise his way into a much bigger part than he was originally hired for, and the fact he pulled it off hilariously led to him getting noticed by Hollywood bigwigs.

174 DRAKE AND
BAKE

Canadian rapper Drake disappointed European fans in 2017 when he canceled a show in Amsterdam, claiming food poisoning. Some sources say that bad sushi was the culprit, but fellow musician DJ Akademiks claimed there was another reason behind the no-show: that Drake had overdosed on marijuana and had a case of the barfs.

175 LEAF LOVER

Canadian actor Jay Baruchel loves his home country so much that he has a maple leaf tattooed over his heart. Another leaf that Baruchel is rather fond of is cannabis, regularly celebrating the unofficial stoner holiday every April 20. There are no reports as to where he has a pot leaf tattooed.

176 DELTA DOPERS

Veteran actor Donald Sutherland became a part of weed history with his portrayal of stoner professor Dave Jennings in *Animal House*. Oddly enough, however, Sutherland reportedly had the least pot knowledge of anyone on set. In an interview with *The Guardian* in 2005, he remembered his confusion when other actors were smoking actual marijuana: "I didn't even know what smoking dope was. I literally didn't know what the smell was. I thought it was smoke-effects stuff for the movie!"

177 LIKELY STORY

Celine Dion may have a squeaky-clean image to her fan base, but that doesn't mean she's never sampled ganja. She was open enough to admit that fact in an interview, recalling a visit to Amsterdam when she sampled the local wares (quickly, before the paparazzi spotted her). She said it...had no effect on her whatsoever: "Nothing. No. But I didn't choke. I took one puff and I said, 'Okay, nothing happened!' It was funny." Uh huh.

178 WELL, DUH

Canadian actress Rachel McAdams revealed on *Jimmy Kimmel Live!* how she used marijuana to treat her insomnia. No doctor recommended it or anything—she said a grocer from the small town where she lives took her aside and slipped her some. After initially resisting the offer, she recalled how she did wind up smoking some, hallucinating, and having thoughts that weren't "normal."

179

WAS SHE STARING
AT HER HAND
THE WHOLE TIME?

Former *Party of Five* actress and Canada native Neve Campbell remains coy about using marijuana in her personal life. Considering the fact her mother is from Amsterdam, she doesn't deny at least some exposure to it. And after she and her *Reefer Madness* costar Alan Cumming gave an interview to *High Times* magazine to promote the project, a representative of the publication observed, "They were definitely smoking pot."

180

IT MAKES FOR A GREAT
BAND NAME

Members of the popular band Green Day aren't so much huge fans of the color as they are of pot. Their original name was Sweet Children when they formed in 1987, but they dropped it in 1988 to avoid confusion with another local band, Sweet Baby. They chose the name Green Day due to their shared appreciation for marijuana. Other not-so-subtle cannabis-supporting bands include Bongwater, High on Fire, Kottonmouth Kings, and Bongzilla.

181 PROBABLY, BUT IT STILL WOULDN'T HAVE HELPED BLUTO'S GRADES

Saturday Night Live alumnus and Canadian comedy hero Dan Aykroyd made an interesting observation about his friend and frequent costar John Belushi in reference to the out-of-control drug habit that wound up ending his life: "If he'd been a pothead, he'd be alive today."

182 SMOKE UP, MCFLY

Canadian film star Michael J. Fox formed a foundation to help fellow Parkinson's disease sufferers called, naturally enough, the Michael J. Fox Foundation. Seeing the possible benefits marijuana might have for Parkinson's sufferers, the foundation has joined a large collection of advocacy organizations in asking the United States government to allow increased research into medical cannabis. Although Fox probably should have thought of a way to solve the problem with Doc Brown back in the 1950s.

183 **UH, NO, THANKS.**

During an interview on Howard Stern's radio show, Canadian rocker Neil Young shared with the infamous shock jock his unusual remedy for the paranoia that often accompanies marijuana use: "Try black pepper balls if you get paranoid. Just chew two or three pieces. I just found this out myself. Try it."

 184 MAYBE THE CAVEMAN LAWYER WAS AN INDICATION

Comedic jack-of-all-trades Phil Hartman may be gone, but the characters the Canadian comedic genius played on *Saturday Night Live* will live forever in TV history. None of those characters, however, really hinted at the life Hartman led before he was a star. A full-blown hippie, he had the long hair, the VW van, and part-time occupation as a rock-band roadie before he made it big in the comedy world. Along with, of course, a lifelong love of marijuana.

185 THE DAILY DOOBIE

Jeopardy! host Alex Trebek hails from Canada, but he now spends his days in Southern California where he attends lavish parties in Malibu, like the one where he unwittingly gobbled down a bunch of hash brownies. As he related to Howard Stern during a radio interview, he had previous experience smoking marijuana to relieve his arthritis, but didn't quite have the tolerance that eating a plateful of weed-filled baked goods requires: "I love chocolate, and I ate four or five hash brownies. The party was on a Friday night…I didn't leave their home until Monday morning."

186 HEAVEN
INDEED

Louisa May Alcott, the author of *Little Women*, was apparently a psychedelic experimenter, as her prose is peppered with references to mind-bending substances. Sometimes they're expressly marijuana, as in her short story "Perilous Play," in which two potential mates eat pot bonbons, which brings them together. "Heaven bless hashish, if its dreams end like this!" reads the story's final line. To which we say, "Amen!"

187 CROONING, CHRONIC,
AND CAKE

Canadian Grammy winner Michael Bublé has a squeaky-clean image onstage, but he absolutely believes marijuana is crucial to his creative process. He's claimed publicly that "I never wrote a song without a bit of a smoke." A former girlfriend's statements might further confirm Bublé's infatuation with weed, as she has described him as a "self-obsessed jerk" whose desires consist solely of "sex, cannabis and cake."

188 BE LIKE DYLAN

Just the mention of Bob Dylan should make you want to light up. In the time of beatniks, Dylan played the local coffeehouses in New York City's Greenwich Village, protesting the war in Vietnam and building a following of peace-loving, like-minded fans. Smoking pot was becoming more popular, and some credit Dylan with turning them on to it. It's even been said Dylan introduced the Beatles to weed.

189 *PINEAPPLE EXPRESS* DESERVED A NOMINATION, AT LEAST

Native Canadian Seth Rogen's relationship with marijuana goes beyond his moviemaking career and personal indulgences. His activism in legalization efforts has been prodigious enough to earn him the *High Times* "Stoner of the Year" award. As an Oscar is unlikely to grace his mantel anytime soon, it's nice that they gave him something to carry under his arm at Hollywood parties.

190 PUNCHING UP

Leading up to Canada's vote on marijuana legalization, late-night talk show host Jimmy Kimmel made a less-than-flattering observation on his TV show. He noted that the law would effectively make the nation "the stoner living in America's attic." But we can feel a sense of justice at the slight, seeing as how at that point, Kimmel's ratings were in the cellar.

191 IN A FIGHT, WE'LL BET ON THE HOCKEY PLAYER

Canadian hockey legend Wayne Gretzky's opinions on marijuana aren't known, but we know for sure that he's definitely against potential sons-in-law smoking it. When Gretzky's daughter became engaged to professional golfer Dustin Johnson, the hockey icon threatened to scuttle the entire thing over numerous positive PGA tests for drugs. However, the fact that the most recent one was for cocaine might have weighed more in his opinions than the 2009 positive test for pot.

192 BE ONE WITH THE BEATS

One of the most prominent of the Beat Generation poets was Allen Ginsberg, who hung around with other big-name Beat writers like William S. Burroughs, John Holmes, and Jack Kerouac, sharing ideas, advice, and an occasional joint. Like many prominent writers of his generation, Ginsberg experimented heavily with drugs in order to expand his mind and allow for more creative thought, and he was a vocal proponent of LSD and marijuana use.

193 TUPAC GOES UP IN SMOKE

Tupac Shakur's former crew, who call themselves the Outlawz, made the rather unsanitary claim that they had rolled his cremated ashes into a blunt and smoked him. You know, out of respect. Shakur's family is curious as to how this could have possibly happened, seeing as how they would never have given permission for such a thing and that his friends would have had to somehow sneak his ashes out from under their noses. Nonetheless, a member of the Outlawz, Young Noble, assured the skeptics that "it's definitely true. We hit the beach and had a little memorial for him with his Moms and family and s**t. We was just givin' him our own farewell...We twisted up some of that great-granddaddy California kush and mixed the big homie with it, ya know what I mean?"

194 HEY, IT'S WORTH A SHOT

The reggae artist Shaggy, whose actual name is Orville Burrell, served in the Gulf War as a US Marine. His current outlook on military tactics seems to have been shaped by his ganja-friendly music career, as he's proposed a rather unorthodox method for dealing with the troubles in the Middle East: "High people don't want to kill nothing; they want to love. They need to bag some Jamaican weed and distribute it amongst ISIS. I guarantee there won't be any more wars out there." Oh, and naturally he proclaims that listening to his records can assist in ending overseas conflicts as well.

195 SNOOP TALES

Because we know you're curious, here, in his own words, is Snoop Dogg's first weed experience: "The first time I got high off marijuana was in the seventies, with one of my uncles. They had these little roaches on the table—these partway-smoked marijuana cigarettes—and there was some Schlitz Malt Liquor Bull. I went in there and sipped the Schlitz, and my uncle asked me did I wanna hit that roach. And I was like, 'Yeah.' He put it on the roach clip for me and lit it up, and I hit that motherfucker. I was about eight or nine years old."

THE REAL GRASSY KNOLL

According to a biography of former US President John F. Kennedy by historian Michael O'Brien, he once smoked weed in the White House. To make it even more of a party, he allegedly did it with a mistress, and just a short while before he was to host a conference on narcotics.

ALL YOU NEED IS WEED

The Beatles' 1965 movie *Help!* was a wanton cavalcade of marijuana consumption, according to members of the band. John Lennon said, "We were smoking marijuana for breakfast…and nobody could communicate with us, because we were just all glazed eyes, giggling all the time. In our own world." And Ringo Starr, when discussing a scene where he and Paul McCartney had to run from a bomb, said, "Paul and I ran about seven miles, we just ran and ran, just so we could stop and have a joint before we came back."

198 A STILL-DEVELOPING SENSE OF HUMOR

It probably won't come as much of a shock to learn that the actor/comedian who played Carl Spackler in *Caddyshack* has dabbled in marijuana at various points in his life. However, Bill Murray has a pretty spectacular tale to tell about the time he was caught with ten pounds of the stuff in his luggage at an airport. He was only twenty years old and catching a flight at O'Hare International in Chicago when he joked with a fellow traveler that he had "two bombs" in his bags. Security was told about the situation, and while they didn't find any explosives, they found the weed, and Murray received five years of probation.

199 YOU CAN BE HIGH AND STILL WIN AN ACADEMY AWARD

Before attending the 1991 Academy Awards, actress Whoopi Goldberg decided to calm her nerves with a harmless joint. While this seemed like a good idea at the time, she immediately regretted the decision when she won the award for best supporting actress for her role in the film *Ghost*. According to Goldberg, she had to mentally coach herself up the stairs and through the process of picking up the statue.

200 AMERICA, F**** YEAH!

During a discussion on marijuana legalization on *Real Time with Bill Maher*, the eponymous host took out what looked exactly like a joint, lit it up, and took a drag. Supposedly, the United States Federal Communications Commission, which oversees all of American TV, responded to this act by fining him $1.7 million. But is this story true? Well, according to Snopes.com, the FCC never actually fined him. But, according to Maher, he did indeed fire up a spliff right on live TV. In a *Twitter* post following the show, he proclaimed, "Yup, that was real last night. And, I think, a first. (Zach's was fake but he paved the way!) America, f*** yeah!" ("Zach" refers to Zach Galifianakis, with whom Maher had smoked a fake joint on his show several years prior.)

201 TEENAGE STONER GROWS UP TO RULE WINTERFELL (BRIEFLY)

Alfie Allen is best known as the actor who plays Theon Greyjoy in the popular HBO series *Game of Thrones*, but many of his fans are not aware that he is also the brother of British pop singer Lily Allen. She even wrote a song for him, titled "Alfie," in which she chastised him for sitting around in his room all day smoking pot.

202 ROCK AND ROLL IS
GREATER THAN THE LAW

In 2010, AC/DC drummer Phil Rudd was found with twenty-five grams of marijuana on a boat he had moored in a New Zealand marina. A judge dropped the charges, however, on the simple grounds that a conviction would have prevented Rudd from touring with the band.

203 DON'T TRY THIS AT HOME

During an "Ask Me Anything" question-and-answer session on the website *Reddit*, musician Snoop Dogg claimed to smoke eighty-one blunts a day, seven days a week. He also confirmed that Willie Nelson was the only person to ever outsmoke him, and revealed he once went 164 days without smoking marijuana. However, he did not reveal at what point in his life he took the hiatus, or why. Maybe he experienced a 164-day long coma before he got famous.

204 THE LEGEND OF PROHIBITION

When entertainer John Legend was interviewed on HuffPost Live, he advocated for America to follow Canada's lead, saying, "I think we need to legalize marijuana. There's no good reason to continue prohibition, and we need to consider ending prohibition in general. I don't know if prohibition has ever been an effective way of getting people not to use banned substances."

205 WAS "JOHN SMITH" TAKEN OR SOMETHING?

Carl Sagan, the noted and beloved astronomer/cosmologist/astrophysicist/all-around nice guy and original host of *Cosmos*, was a big proponent of the legalization of marijuana. You may very well know that. But it only recently came to light that he was also an outspoken advocate in secret, writing many articles under the most unoriginal pseudonym of all time, Mr. X. For someone so smart, you'd think he'd come up with something better.

206 HIGHER CONSCIOUSNESS

Richard Feynman, the Nobel Prize–winning theoretical physicist, credits much of his success in his study of human consciousness to his experimentation with marijuana. He said he used it to "get a hallucination going," which he credits with greatly helping his work.

207 I YAM WHAT I TOKE?

The evidence is purely circumstantial, but there are many who believe the cartoon character Popeye's uncontrollable spinach addiction may be a reference to marijuana. Back in the late twenties when he was created, rumors were floating around that pot could give you superhuman strength and "spinach" was considered a slang term for marijuana, so it's not totally out of the question.

208 SCOOBY-DOOBY-DOO

It's long been supposed that Shaggy and Scoob from the cartoon *Scooby-Doo* were stoners, but the live-action "kids'" movie all but confirmed it. When Shaggy Rogers, as played by Matthew Lillard, is on an airplane, he meets a girl who shares his love for Scooby Snacks. She notes that they're "100 percent vegetarian" and introduces herself as Mary Jane, to which Shaggy exclaims, "Like, that is my favorite name!"

209 EVIL DANK

During filming of the classic horror movie *The Evil Dead*, there was a scene planned where the characters would sit around listening to an old recording while smoking weed. When the actors decided to get super high on actual marijuana, however, they reportedly became so rowdy and "unruly" that the scene had to be scrapped, and any trace of pot was removed from the film entirely.

210 TAKING THE "GREEN ROOM" TOO LITERALLY

As actors often do to promote their films, Paul Rudd and Jason Segel went on a press tour after making their film *I Love You, Man*. While they've never confirmed the rumors, it's believed that they smoked copious amounts of marijuana before sitting down for an interview with a British journalist. It's hard to argue for their sobriety when you see the video, and the silliness on display has been described as "an altered state of joy for almost everyone involved."

211 C'MON BABY, LIGHT MY JOINT

Like most bands of the sixties, the Doors smoked a lot of weed. Their music represented both the calm and soothing effects of smoking and the angry, rebellious times of that era. The Doors got into a heap of trouble while on *The Ed Sullivan Show*, when they refused to change one of the lyrics to remove a drug reference and Morrison sang "Girl we couldn't get much higher." Needless to say, Eddie was not happy and banned them from the show.

212 PASS THE JOINT, SCOTTY

The fact that there's a popular cannabis strain called "Romulan" isn't the only *Star Trek*–related pot factoid out there. William Shatner, Captain Kirk himself, has professed his admiration for the "great herb." On his web show *Brown Bag Wine Tasting*, the octogenarian Star Fleet Commander stated quite frankly, "Oh, I love marijuana."

213 SOME LIKE IT DANK

A short video recently emerged purportedly showing cinema icon Marilyn Monroe in a New Jersey home, toking away on a marijuana joint with some friends. There are skeptics who say it's not what it seems to be, but it wouldn't exactly be a huge surprise, what with her hard-partying ways. What is somewhat of a shock is that the clip, which was hidden away in an attic for decades, sold immediately for $275,000.

214 DIFF'RENT TOKES

Diff'rent Strokes, the family sitcom from the eighties, became known for two things during its eight-year run: Arnold's catchphrase "What you talkin' 'bout, Willis?" and their "very special" episodes. In "First Day Blues," Willis is coerced by some kids at school to buy them some weed because he's rich, and he does it because he's desperate for friends. But when Dad finds out, he flushes Willis's weed down the toilet, warning him, "If I ever even hear you going near that junk again, I will take you to the police station myself."

215 STRONG CHONG

Tommy Chong (of the comedy duo Cheech and Chong, obviously) has survived two cancer scares, and gives kudos to his marijuana habit for helping his appetite return after chemotherapy. It seems he needed the munchies so he could lift weights to get his strength back, and ultimately disgrace himself by appearing on *Dancing with the Stars*.

216 PETER "POTHEAD" GRIFFIN

Family Guy is a classic stoner show, but sadly, creator Seth MacFarlane has sworn off Mary Jane. He says, "I don't smoke much pot anymore. One of the last times I was stoned, I was convinced that I would die unless I kept moving my body. So I sat there, baked, waving my arms around like a crazy person." Dude, what's wrong with crazy?

217 THAT EXPLAINS
THE TREE OF LIFE

Brad Pitt was outed as a stoner by a head-shop owner in Los Angeles, who said the actor used to come into the shop and buy decorative bongs for his coworkers and "it seemed like all he wanted to do was smoke weed, make movies, and go to the beach." Comedian Bill Maher also claimed Pitt rolled the most perfect joints at a party the two attended. Handsome, talented, rich, and an expert joint roller. Life's not fair.

218 FAIR WEATHER
FRIENDS

In an effort to be taken more seriously, the American National Cannabis Industry Association decided to disassociate itself from legendary, weed-friendly comedians Cheech and Chong, who were supporters of their cause. According to an announcement, the organization's goal was to "move past the stoner stereotypes" and become more respected members of the economic community.

 219 WHOLESOME
FAMILY FUN

Barry Williams, the actor who played Greg Brady in *The Brady Bunch*, revealed in his autobiography *Growing Up Brady* how he showed up for work one day stoned completely out of his gourd. In case you'd like to look it up, the episode in question was called "Law and Disorder," which is notable for Williams almost tripping over a bicycle pump, staring into space, and ad-libbing "far out" in the middle of a scene.

WHAT A
 220 JACKASS

Jackass's Steve-O (real name Stephen Glover) made the news when he was arrested for smuggling pot into Sweden during his "Don't Try This at Home" tour. He was caught when he boasted to local media that he'd swallowed a condom filled with pot and was basically waiting for it to make an appearance so he could smoke it. He ended up paying a $6,700 fine and was good to go.

221 NOT A BLATANT CASH GRAB WHATSOEVER

Reality TV star Bethenny Frankel is attempting to parlay her *Real Housewives of New York City* fame into profiting from the lucrative recreational cannabis field. Her product, Skinnygirl Marijuana, purports to be a strain of weed that's mysteriously designed to not give people the munchies. It seems something of a dubious claim, but hey, if you can't trust reality TV stars, who can you trust?

222 CATATONIC COUNTRY

Willie Nelson is synonymous with both country music and weed, and to pay tribute to his legendary status, fellow musicians Toby Keith and Scotty Emerick wrote and recorded a song titled "Weed with Willie." It recalls a time they hung out with Nelson backstage at a Farm Aid concert, when they all passed around one of his "fat boys." The experience left the novice tokers drooling in the fetal position with a solemn oath to "never smoke weed with Willie again."

223 SPACE COWBOY

It usually doesn't come as much of a surprise to hear a famous actor likes to indulge in a little THC TLC every now and again. Even the late James Garner, the award-winning actor known for his serious roles in films such as *The Great Escape* and *The Notebook*, revealed he'd smoked marijuana for much of his adult life: "I started smoking it in my late teens. I drank to get drunk but ultimately didn't like the effect. Not so with grass. It had the opposite effect from alcohol: it made me more tolerant and forgiving...I smoked marijuana for fifty years and I don't know where I'd be without it."

224 TOKER FACE

Lady Gaga is regarded as one of the most creative people in the American music industry. When asked in a *60 Minutes* interview how she comes up with her catchy tunes, she replied, "I smoke a lot of pot when I write music." They failed to ask her what she took to come up with the famed meat dress she wore in 2010.

225 A SMOKE-FILLED HOMAGE

Jerry Seinfeld's comedy web series *Comedians in Cars Getting Coffee* was a pretty darn good idea, enough for someone to take the basic premise and insert a little marijuana into the mix. Seattle writer Michael A. Stusser has made a similar show to Seinfeld's, with just that aforementioned tweak, and called it *Comedians in Cars Smoking Cannabis*.

226 MARIJUANA ON MY MIND

Just in case you need any more convincing that Willie Nelson is an enthusiastic fan of weed, he released a song called "Roll Me Up and Smoke Me When I Die." It was released on 4/20, naturally, and the video featured cameos by a slew of fellow pothead musicians, including Kris Kristofferson and Snoop Dogg.

 HIT ONE OUT
OF THE PARK

Orlando Cepeda, the Hall of Fame baseball player, had a long and storied career. Not just in baseball, but in marijuana too. In 1966, he unsuccessfully tried to smuggle 160—yes, one-six-zero—pounds of marijuana from Puerto Rico to Miami. In 1978, he was sentenced to ten years in prison on drug possession charges before settling down and becoming a goodwill ambassador for the game of baseball.

 SHUT UP AND
SMOKE THAT

Bill Hicks, the legendary comic from the eighties, was a big fan of marijuana. Many of his most famous jokes were centered around pot. Though he died before it came to pass, he envisioned a utopia with legal weed, saying, "That would be a nice world, wouldn't it? Quiet, mellow, hungry, high people everywhere. Domino's pizza trucks everywhere."

229 ON THE REEFER ROAD

Let's be honest: if you're thinking about drug-using writers, Jack Kerouac will always be at the top of the list. Since his death in 1969, his drug-soaked novel *On the Road* has become a bible for free spirits everywhere. Kerouac often wrote under the influence of marijuana and coined the term "Beat Generation," which is characterized by, among many other things, the advocacy of decriminalizing marijuana and other drugs.

230 OLD-SCHOOL STONER

Revered in cannabis circles and beyond as a standup legend, George Carlin talked pot in a *Playboy* interview that dates back to 1982. Can you dig it? "I was a stonehead for thirty years. I'd wake up in the morning and if I couldn't decide whether I wanted to smoke a joint or not, I'd smoke a joint to figure it out. And I stayed high all day long. When people asked me, 'Do you get high to go onstage?' I could never understand the question. I mean, I'd been high since eight that morning. Going onstage had nothing to do with it."

231 NATURAL BORN SMOKERS

Woody Harrelson, first introduced to the world as the innocent and lovable Woody Boyd in *Cheers*, is a huge supporter and activist for the legalization of marijuana and hemp in America. With fame comes attention, and he's seen his fair share of trouble concerning his views on pot. He was once arrested in Kentucky after he planted four hemp seeds. He did this to challenge the state law that did not distinguish between industrial hemp and marijuana. Harrelson actually won the case and it was a big victory for the weed-smoking community.

232 DAZED AND SERIOUSLY CONFUSED

Picture this: an A-list actor found screaming like a banshee, playing the bongos, and completely naked. Just another day in the life of Matthew McConaughey. He was once arrested at his home after someone called the police reporting a disturbance. He was in possession of marijuana, but he denied the drug charges and was only charged with disturbing the peace. You've probably done some crazy things while high, but McConaughey has to be the first to play the bongos, naked, loud enough for the cops to be called.

233 VAMPIRES WITH THE MUNCHIES: BAD COMBINATION

Kristen Stewart, who played Bella Swan in *Twilight*, isn't as innocent as the character she played. Kristen was seen taking a hit off of a pipe while sitting on the steps of her house. She's also been photographed wearing a pot leaf bikini. Can you really blame her though? Being a vampire's girlfriend can't be all it's cracked up to be.

JACK BLACK: THE EMBODIMENT OF CANNABIS CLASSINESS

As a past recipient of the "Smoker of the Year" award by *High Times*, Jack Black has done much of his best work in the "stoner comedy" genre. However, when asked about how often he smokes in an interview with Maxim.com, Jack Black said, "It's basically limited to celebratory Js on special occasions. I did smoke the other day before a meeting, and it was a big mistake. I'm a lightweight, and if I smoke really powerful weed, I get paranoid and nonverbal."

235 AN APPLE A DAY

Charlize Theron is not only drop-dead gorgeous, but she also loves to smoke up. She was photographed smoking out of a homemade apple bong in her backyard and then having a giggling fit. The star of *Mad Max: Fury Road* hasn't commented publicly on her love of smoking, but making an apple bong takes some serious stoner ingenuity.

236 YOUR DRUG DEALER MIGHT GROW UP TO BE FAMOUS

Rapper Snoop Dogg and actress Cameron Diaz are both advocates of marijuana use, and actually grew up together and attended the same high school. Although she is not 100 percent clear on the details, Diaz even claims to have purchased marijuana from Snoop at some point in her youth. Snoop admits, "I might have sold her some of that white-girl weed."

 237 MAYBE NOT THE BEST ADVICE...

In an interview with the host of Comedy Central's *The Daily Show with Jon Stewart*, famed pothead (and actor) Seth Rogen encouraged kids to drop out of school, smoke a lot of weed, and write a movie about it. I mean, if it worked for him, it can work for you. He makes it sound so easy...

 238 LORD OF THE PIPE

How else would someone come up with Middle-earth, Mordor, and Orcs if they weren't smoking some fine sheeba? J.R.R. Tolkien even made mention of smoking in the text of The Lord of the Rings. In the film and books, one of the hobbits' main hobbies is getting together with friends and smoking "pipe-weed." Also in one scene, the wizard Saruman criticizes Gandalf for smoking too much. He says, "Your love of the halflings' leaf has clearly slowed your mind." Tolkien himself loved a good, packed pipe. Now, whether it was filled with straight tobacco or something else, we'll never know.

 239 EVERGREEN, INDEED

Who knew that Babs liked to get high? Barbra Streisand did an interview for *Rolling Stone* in 1972 in which she admitted to smoking joints onstage. She said she got nervous under the Vegas lights so she'd "take out a joint and light it. First, just faking it. Then I started lighting live joints, passing them around to the band, you know. It was great; it relieved all my tensions." She might not have become a toker for life, but like any good citizen of the seventies, she did her fair share.

 240 THE BONG OLYMPICS

Michael Phelps became the Olympic golden child in the summer of 2008 when he won a record-breaking eight gold medals in swimming. Then he was busted for smoking a bong. Phelps did some quick damage control, saying, "I engaged in behavior which was regrettable and demonstrated bad judgment." USA Swimming hit him with a three-month suspension but he went on to set the record for most medals ever won by an Olympian. If you think about it, he deserves additional medals if he was high while swimming.

241 M-E-T-H-O-D MAN!

He may be a member of the Wu-Tang Clan and half of the rap duo Method Man and Redman, but that doesn't mean he's above the law. Method Man was pulled over by a New York City police officer near NYC's Battery Tunnel. When he rolled down his window, the smell of marijuana was unmistakable. A source quoted in the *Daily News* (New York) described the scene as being "like something out of Cheech and Chong." The officer also saw blunts and marijuana sitting on the passenger seat. Method Man was arrested but managed to avoid jail time by agreeing to do public service announcements warning about the "dangers" of smoking pot.

242 THE FAMOUS SKY-HIGH HOOK

You know Kareem Abdul-Jabbar as one of the greatest basketball players of all time. But did you know that he's also a pothead? According to Abdul-Jabbar's autobiography *Giant Steps*, he first tried pot at the age of seventeen. He called it "one of his first major individual decisions," and apparently spent a lot of time at the library researching marijuana before smoking that first time. What a nerd.

"I AM THE WALRUS" EVEN STARTS TO MAKE SENSE

243

Individually, the Beatles all made news with their marijuana use. Collectively, the band made news in the summer of 1967 when they, along with more than sixty other prominent members of British society, signed a full-page ad in *The Times* (London) newspaper titled "The law against marijuana is immoral in principle and unworkable in practice." Marijuana laws in the UK haven't changed too much, but at least they tried, right?

244 A ROYAL DEBACLE

You'd think it would take more than reefer to send the royal family into a tizzy after all they've been through, but that wasn't the case in 2002. After a staff member of Prince Charles told him about a strong smell of marijuana coming from Prince Harry's room, Charles confronted his son, who admitted to smoking weed. Prince Charles nipped the drug use in the bud (so to speak) and made Harry attend a one-day rehab program where he was taught all about the dangers of substance abuse.

245 AL GORE IS SUCH A FOLLOWER

Hey, if former US President Bill Clinton can admit to smoking pot, why wouldn't his second-in-command Al Gore want to jump on that bandwagon? Actually, Gore admitted his marijuana use in 1987 when he was basically outed by John Warnecke, Gore's former friend and colleague. Obviously, this breaking news didn't affect Gore too much. He's now an environmental activist, and God knows you don't care if he smoked a fat one.

FIVE

CHRONIC QUOTES

Marijuana has inundated our culture. Everyone has an opinion about it these days and they all want to be heard. The best way to get a solid feel for how a society stands on the issue of marijuana isn't by reviewing the current laws on the books, but rather by asking the citizens them-selves. So here is what people are saying about weed.

 COMEDY PROPS

Canada rocks. Primo weed. Really good Chinese food.

—Allison Janney as Ms. Greenstein, *Weeds*

 THE FAILED EXPERIMENT

The legalization of marijuana is not a dangerous experiment—prohibition is the experiment, and it has failed dramatically, with millions of victims all around the world.

—Sebastian Marincolo, author of *High: Insights on Marijuana*

 AT LEAST HE DIDN'T SAY "ON FLEEK"

We're in Canada and the hydroponic stuff up here is just thorough!

—Edward Norton, actor

249 MCCONAUGHEY'S
EASIEST ROLE EVER

Wooderson: Say man, you got a joint?

Mitch: Uhhh, no. Not on me, man.

Wooderson: It'd be a lot cooler if you did.

—Matthew McConaughey as Wooderson and
Wiley Wiggins as Mitch, *Dazed and Confused*

250 SO IT
GOES

Alcohol and marijuana, if used in moderation, plus loud, usually low-class music, make stress and boredom infinitely more bearable.

—Kurt Vonnegut, author

251 THE NEW KING OF
MORNING COMEDY

Researchers have discovered that chocolate produces some of the same reactions in the brain as marijuana. The researchers also discovered other similarities between the two, but can't remember what they are.

—Matt Lauer, TV show host

252 ALSO, LESS
BURPING

I don't consider weed to be any worse than having a beer.

—James Franco, actor

253 CALL IT
MEGADOPE

I'd get up in the morning, wake and bake, watch MTV, sing along with the Buggles, play some guitar, take a nap, and get on with the day. No harm, no foul.

—Dave Mustaine, musician

254 THE POT PLATOON

I went to Vietnam, and I was there for a long time. [Using marijuana] made the difference between staying human or, as Michael Douglas said, becoming a beast. I'm telling you, it's rough and a lot of people in that platoon used it, not on the front line but in the back, to stay in touch with themselves. So, I look at that time in my life as really much of a lifesaver.

—Oliver Stone, film director

255 THE WORLD'S CLASSIEST POTHEAD

A girl and a guy were smoking joints, and they had them in their hands like this [demonstrates holding a joint], and I said boy, those are sloppy joints....Of course I know how to roll a joint.

—Martha Stewart, businesswoman and TV personality

256 WHATEVER YOU SAY, GOD

Never give up the ganja.

—Morgan Freeman, actor

257 JAGGED LITTLE LEAF

If ever I need some clarity...or a quantum leap in terms of writing something, [weed's] a quick way for me to get to it.

—Alanis Morissette, musician

258 BETTER ALL AROUND

Smoking's a way to let you down slowly from a ballgame. It also makes you use less of the resources around. It makes people better in the way they act towards society. Everybody's nicer. It's hard to be mean when you're stoned.

—Bill Lee, American baseball player

259 THE HUNGER GAMES

They said that marijuana was a performance-enhancing drug. Marijuana enhances many things—colors, tastes, sensations, but you are certainly not f**king empowered. When you're stoned, you're lucky if you can find your own goddamn feet. The only way it's a performance-enhancing drug is if there's a big f**king Hershey bar at the end of the run.

—Robin Williams, comedian

260 MIXED MARTIAL MARIJUANA

Actually, on the contrary, my fight career has gotten in the way of my marijuana smoking.

—Nick Diaz, mixed martial artist

261 GOOD LORD... JUST SAY IT'S FUN BEING HIGH

One's condition on marijuana is always existential. One can feel the importance of each moment and how it is changing one. One feels one's being, one becomes aware of the enormous apparatus of nothingness—the hum of a hi-fi set, the emptiness of a pointless interruption, one becomes aware of the war between each of us, how the nothingness in each of us seeks to attack the being of others, how our being in turn is attacked by the nothingness in others.

—Norman Mailer, author

262 LET IT BE

I support decriminalization. People are smoking pot anyway and to make them into criminals is wrong. It's when you're in jail that you really become a criminal. That's where you learn all the tricks.

—Sir Paul McCartney, musician

263 DON'T ANSWER THAT

Marijuana is not a drug. I used to suck dick for coke....You ever suck *dick* for marijuana?

—Bob Saget as Cocaine Addict, *Half Baked*

264 JUST ONCE

Just hit the blunt one time and see if it don't change your perception on what's important in your life.

—Katt Williams, comedian

265 UNTENABLE
TYRANNY!

It is a new form of tyranny by the old over the young. You have the adult with a cocktail in one hand and a cigarette in the other saying, "you cannot" to the child. This is untenable.

—Margaret Mead, cultural anthropologist

266 IT'S ALWAYS EARLY-MID-LATE-EARLY-MORNING SOMEWHERE

I'll be honest with you. I used to smoke...marijuana. But I would only smoke it...in the late evening. Oh, occasionally, the early evening, or mid-evening. But that was it—the late evening, the early evening, or mid-evening, but that was it, I—ohhh, occasionally, the early morning...or, oh, the mid-morning...maybe the late morning...or, occasionally, the early-mid-late morning! Or, sometimes, the mid-early morning, or...oh, the late afternoon! Sometimes, the mid-early-late afternoon! Never at *dusk*! *Noooooo*, I would never smoke it at dusk!

—Steve Martin, comedian

267 DON'T YOU WISH YOUR DAD WAS MORE LIKE THIS GUY?

I think pot should be legal. I don't smoke it, but I like the smell of it.

—Andy Warhol, artist

268 WHAT A WONDERFUL WORLD

It really puzzles me to see marijuana connected with narcotics…dope and all that crap. It's a thousand times better than whiskey. It's an assistant—a friend.

—Louis Armstrong, musician

269 THE ALL-SEEING HERB

When you smoke the herb, it reveals you to yourself.

—Bob Marley, musician

 270 THE WEED DIARY

I have always loved marijuana. It has been a source of joy and comfort to me for many years. And I still think of it as a basic staple of life, along with beer and ice and grapefruits—and millions of Americans agree with me.

—Hunter S. Thompson, writer

 271 SAFER THAN POTATOES?

In strict medical terms marijuana is far safer than many foods we commonly consume. For example, eating ten raw potatoes can result in a toxic response. By comparison, it is physically impossible to eat enough marijuana to induce death....Marijuana, in its natural form, is one of the safest therapeutically active substances known to man. By any measure of rational analysis marijuana can be safely used within the supervised routine of medical care.

—Francis Young, former US Drug Enforcement Agency chief administrative law judge

272 · EVEN OUR NERDIEST SMOKE POT

As for drugs—well, [Bill] Gates was certainly not unusual there. Marijuana was the pharmaceutical of choice.

—Stephen Manes and Paul Andrews in *Gates: How Microsoft's Mogul Reinvented an Industry—And Made Himself the Richest Man in America*

273 · WHAT ABOUT CORNED BEEF?

What is the different types of hash out there? We all know that it's called the bionic, the bomb, the puff, the blow, the black, the herb, the sensie, the chronic, the sweet Mary Jane, the shit, ganja, split, reefa, the bad, the buddha, the home grown, the ill, the maui-maui, the method, pot, lethal turbo, tie, shake, skunk, stress, wacky, weed, glaze, the boot, dime-bag, Scooby-Doo, bob, bogey, back yard boogie. But what is the other terms for it?

—Sacha Baron Cohen as Ali G, *Da Ali G Show*

274 THE MERITS OF
BEING LAZY

They lie about marijuana. Tell you pot smoking makes you unmotivated. Lie! When you're high, you can do everything you normally do just as well— you just realize that it's not worth the f***ing effort. There is a difference.

—Bill Hicks, comedian

275 EVERYTHING IS
BETTER

It makes everything better. Makes food better, makes music better, makes sex feel better, for God's sake. It makes shitty movies better, you know?

—Seth Rogen as Dale Denton, *Pineapple Express*

276 DEEP THINKING AT DELTA HOUSE

Pinto: OK, so that means that our whole solar system could be like one tiny atom in the fingernail of some other giant being. This is nuts! That means that one tiny atom in my fingernail could be...

Professor Jennings: ...could be one tiny little universe.

Pinto: Can I buy some pot from you?

—Tom Hulce as Larry "Pinto" Kroger and Donald Sutherland as Professor Dave Jennings, *Animal House*

277 HIGH JINX, INDEED

The amount of money and of legal energy being given to prosecute hundreds of thousands of Americans who are caught with a few ounces of marijuana in their jeans simply makes no sense—the kindest way to put it. A sterner way to put it is that it is an outrage, an imposition on basic civil liberties and on the reasonable expenditure of social energy.

—William F. Buckley Jr., author

278 THE FINEST OF INTOXICANTS

Marijuana is quite possibly the finest of intoxicants. It has been scientifically proven, for decades, to be much less harmful to the body than alcohol when used on a regular basis.

—Nick Offerman, actor

 THERE'S HAPPINESS IN FILTH

279

The Scythians take kannabis seed, creep in under the felts, and throw it on the red-hot stones. It smolders and sends up such billows of steam-smoke that no Greek vapor bath can surpass it. The Scythians howl with joy in these vapor-baths, which serve them instead of bathing, for they never wash their bodies with water.

—Herodotus, Greek historian of the fifth century B.C.E.

 *SO* WORTH IT

280

Is marijuana addictive? Yes, in the sense that most of the really pleasant things in life are worth endlessly repeating.

—Richard Neville, author

281 HITTING THE
HIGH NOTES

We smoked a joint and snorted a line before every session—a CSN ritual. It put us in a rapturous mood.

—Graham Nash, musician

282 THE SOCIOLOGY OF
SMOKING UP

It should tell us something that in healthy societies drug use is celebrative, convivial, and occasional, whereas among us it is lonely, shameful, and addictive. We need drugs, apparently, because we have lost each other.

—Wendell Berry, author

283 DON'T GIVE THEM ANY IDEAS

People say you can abuse marijuana. Well shit, you can abuse cheeseburgers too, you know? You don't go around closing Burger King because you can abuse something.

—Joe Rogan, comedian

284 DO IT FOR THE GOATS

Birds eat it
Ants love it
Fowls eat it
Goats love to play with it
So you've got to legalize it
And don't criticize it
Legalize it, yeah
And I will advertise it.

—Peter Tosh, musician, "Legalize It"

 285 HE'S A FAN OF WEED, YOU COULD SAY

I could smoke weed every second of every day.

—Jonah Hill as Jonah, *Knocked Up*

 286 THE MAGICAL MARIJUANA MIRROR

The brain on marijuana will never deviate from its destined disposition, nor be driven to madness. Marijuana is a mirror reflecting man's deepest thoughts, a magnifying mirror. It's true, but only ever a mirror.

—Charles Baudelaire, nineteenth-century French poet

287 HE SPEAKS THE TRUTH

Facing reality is easier when you are high.

—Jackie Robinson, baseball player

288 SOUNDS LIKE A GREAT TIME

One time, my group, the Upright Citizens Brigade, got to host the Cannabis Cup in Amsterdam. I don't remember much of it.

—Amy Poehler, actress and comedian

289 THAT MAKES... SENSE?

To be just without being mad (and the madder you get, the madder you get), to be peaceful without being stupid, to be interested without being compulsive, to be happy without being hysterical...smoke grass.

—Ken Kesey, author

290 WHAT HAPPENS WHEN YOU RING A BELL?

Pavlov's pothead...I hear the sound of a bong clink and my eyes begin to water.

—Kieran Culkin as Igby, *Igby Goes Down*

291 SO THAT EXPLAINS
THE NEWTON MESSAGEPAD

The best way I would describe the effect of the marijuana and the hashish is that it would make me relaxed and creative.

—Steve Jobs, businessman and inventor

292 NIRVANA
INDEED

We found the hippie holy grail, a government-sponsored dope store that served tea and snacks.

—Tom Davis, *Thirty-Nine Years of Short-Term Memory Loss: The Early Days of SNL from Someone Who Was There*

293 DON'T DO IT, DEWEY!

Dewey Cox: What are y'all doin' in here?

Sam: We're smoking reefer and you don't want no part of this shit...

Dewey Cox: You know what, I don't want no hangover. I can't get no hangover.

Sam: It doesn't give you a hangover!

Dewey Cox: Wha—I get addicted to it or something?

Sam: It's not habit-forming!

Dewey Cox: Oh, okay...well, I don't know...I don't want to overdose on it.

Sam: You can't OD on it!

Dewey Cox: It's not gonna make me wanna have sex, is it?

Sam: It makes sex even better!

Dewey Cox: Sounds kind of expensive.

Sam: It's the cheapest drug there is...you don't want it.

Dewey Cox: I think I kinda want it.

Sam: Okay, just this once. Come on in.

—John C. Reilly as Dewey Cox and Tim Meadows as Sam, *Walk Hard: The Dewey Cox Story*

MAYBE IN THE FUTURE
294 JUST LISTEN
AND NOT TALK

Greg Focker: [in the car listening to "Puff the Magic Dragon"] Who would've thought it wasn't really about a dragon, huh?

Jack Byrnes: What do you mean?

Greg Focker: You know, the whole drug thing?

Jack Byrnes: No, I don't know. Why don't you tell me?

Greg Focker: Some people think that to "puff the magic dragon" means to—They're really, uh—to smoke—to smoke—a marijuana cigarette.

Jack Byrnes: Puff's just the name of the boy's magical dragon.

Greg Focker: Right.

Jack Byrnes: Are you a pothead, Focker?

Greg Focker: No! No. What? No, no, no, no, Jack. No, I'm—I'm not—I—I pass on grass all the time. I mean, not all the time.

Jack Byrnes: Yes or no, Greg?

Greg Focker: No. Yes. No.

—Robert De Niro as Jack Byrnes and Ben Stiller as Greg Focker, *Meet the Parents*

295 THAT EXPLAINS THE HAND-STARING

When you're high on pot, you see detail. The detail could just be a nice day, or a flower, or it could be a little kid playing in the park. You focus on the little details, and that's what makes it so valuable for artists—because we focus on detail. We don't just see the one thing, we see and hear everything.

—Tommy Chong, actor

296 DRUG-FREE LIFESTYLE

I don't do drugs though. Just weed.

—Dave Chappelle as Thurgood Jenkins, *Half Baked*

 297 WELL, THAT IS PRETTY BAD

They have done study after study after study on this issue of marijuana—every administration since, like, FDR. You know what they found out? It makes you want to eat SpaghettiOs right out of the saucepan. That's the worst thing.

—Bill Maher, comedian

 298 SMOKEY MAKES A GOOD POINT

I know you don't smoke weed. I know this. But I'm going to get you high today 'cause it's Friday. You ain't got no job, and you ain't got shit to do.

—Chris Tucker as Smokey, *Friday*

299 JUST ACT NORML

When pop culture began to embrace marijuana, to treat it either in a humorous fashion or kinda an ordinary fashion...you knew we were making progress because popular culture mimics, to some extent, changes that are already going on.

—Keith Stroup, founder of the National Organization for the Reform of Marijuana Laws in the US

300 IT'S A WONDERFUL LIFE (WHEN YOU'RE HIGH, ANYWAY)

For centuries, marijuana has been used as a self-prescribed remedy for the terminal disease known as "being alive."

—Steve Carell, comedian,
The Daily Show with Jon Stewart

301 I LOVE DRUGS! WELL... ACTUALLY JUST ONE

I have to be honest; I have contempt for pretty much every drug other than pot. I find drunk people gross. Most people with more than one drink in them aren't giggly, goofy, and happy the way people are with a puff of pot smoke in them....At a party, I have so much fun stoned, flitting about—but once I sniff that first wave of drunkenness on someone, I'm out of there.

—Sarah Silverman, comedian, *The Bedwetter: Stories of Courage, Redemption, and Pee*

302 SO IT ENDED UP BEING GREAT

As usual, marijuana saves an otherwise disastrous day.

—Elden Henson as Pnub, *Idle Hands*

303 WELL, OBVIOUSLY

Music and herb go together. It's been a long time now I smoke herb. From 1960s, when I first start singing.

—Bob Marley, musician

304 NINE OUT OF TEN DOCTORS RECOMMEND

I've been smoking pot all my life. I've found it tremendously relaxing. I do it a lot. The doctor told me, "Don't smoke cigarettes. Just smoke pot."

—Rodney Dangerfield, comedian, *Live from New York: The Complete, Uncensored History of* Saturday Night Live

305 JUST SAY NO TO CHO'S DOUGH

I'm not afraid of a gang of red-eyed, cotton-mouthed, paranoid stoners coming to jack me for my Visine and cookie dough.

—Margaret Cho, comedian

306 HAPPY HOUR

Like a lot of other people, I've smoked marijuana. It is what goes on in this country. [In the early 1970s], I thought it was a mind-expanding experience, just like a lot of kids and a lot of adults do. Most people who smoke marijuana do it in a way similar to having cocktails in the evening.

—Gary Johnson, former governor
of the state of New Mexico

307 VICTORY GARDENS

I guess you guys are too busy to be bothered by things like mosquito bites. I hear you go in for gardening. The commanding officer says you grow your own grass....In one barracks I passed, a group of GIs was watching "Twelve O'Clock High" and they didn't even have a TV set.

—Bob Hope, comedian, to the American troops,
Bob Hope: A Tribute

SIX

POT-FRIENDLY PRODUCTS

Cannabis has directly led to some great innovations in just about every field. The fact that so many people like smoking weed means it has also led to a cavalcade of bizarre products that might sound like a perfectly sound investment if you're stoned out of your gourd. And now that pot is legal, entrepreneurs and craftspeople are discovering niches to fill that would have seemed almost unthinkable just a few short years ago. Or were just too silly to consider, like…

 THEY CAN
DO IT

Canadian women who are looking to get into the myriad business opportunities that cannabis offers now have a valuable resource at their disposal: Women Grow. This networking group started in the US, but has expanded to include chapters in major cities across the Great White North. It helps female entrepreneurs figure out and navigate the rapidly changing legal landscapes across the continent.

 CURDS AND
CHRONIC

Around the same time Canada announced its plans to legalize weed, the fast food restaurant Carl's Jr. revealed its plan to add a Poutine Burger to its Canadian-only menu. In an advertisement announcing the burger, the burger was described as having a "charbroiled 100 percent Black Angus Beef Patty, Criss-Cut Fries, Cheese Curds, Poutine Gravy, Peppercorn Bacon and Potato Chips. #TrulyCanadian." Coincidence? We think not.

310 THE BLUE
"Js"

A lot of professional sports teams celebrate St. Patrick's Day by adding a touch of green to their uniforms. But not every team has a gigantic leaf as part of their logo, as do the Toronto Blue Jays. When they unveiled their "St. Patty's Diamond Era" caps to commemorate the holiday, wearers wound up looking less like supporters of a baseball team and more like they were proudly displaying their love of the sweet, sweet ganja.

I'LL HAVE SOME JERKWEED

311

A company called Badfish Extracts has come up with a combination that you never knew you really, really wanted: beef jerky infused with pot. Thank goodness they made this responsible choice, as creating a similar concoction involving Timbits would surely have resulted in an alarming spike in the nation's obesity rate.

SMOKABLE ART

312

Tony Greenhand is a twentysomething artist whose chosen medium is weed. That particular professional niche might seem to be a tough sell to some, but apparently Mr. Greenhand can fetch up to $7,000 per piece. And "piece" seems like a rather accurate description of what he makes, since one of his latest creations was an arsenal of massive joints made to look like guns.

 BAKED
BEES

Teaching bees to make honey from marijuana has long been the dream of...somebody, I guess. Anyway, somebody's managed to do it. A beekeeper named Nicolas Trainerbees (alas, only a nickname; his actual last name is just Trainer) in France has coerced the hapless insects in his apiary to collect marijuana resin and produce "cannahoney."

 PRACTICE SAFE
SIZZURP

A couple of years back, a beverage company in California named Actabliss began marketing a "healthy alternative" to the favorite beverage of rappers everywhere: sizzurp. Calling their product "Grape Syzurp with Cannabinoids," complete with a little "Rx" on the label, they removed the codeine from sizzurp's normal list of ingredients and replaced it with THC. The contents are described as "purple and gooey," which sounds somewhat less than delightful. Nevertheless, it's been so popular they're reportedly having trouble keeping up with demand.

315 DEEP-TISSUE
DANK

The LoDo Massage Studio in Colorado offers something called "The Mile High Massage." This is a rubdown that incorporates THC into the massage lotions you can choose to have squirted onto your back. They assure us that "as the THC does not enter the bloodstream, there are no psychoactive effects—just soothing, cooling sensations and immediate relief from pain."

 **316** AN APPRECIATION
FOR THE ARTS

While classical isn't generally considered the preferred musical genre of the stoner community, members of the Colorado Symphony hoped to change that by hosting a series of marijuana-friendly concerts. For each concert in the "High Note Series," the lucky adults who were offered invitations were encouraged to bring their own cannabis and indulge to their hearts' content while the orchestra serenaded them with pieces by Bach, Debussy, and Wagner.

 **317** CANNABIS
CONNOISSEURS

Any fool can stuff pot into a brownie or gobble it down at a moment's notice when a parental figure pounds on his bedroom door. But to truly appreciate the nuanced flavor possibilities of marijuana, dedicated foodies should enlist the service of a gourmet chef. Luckily, marijuana legalization in Colorado has opened the door to weed-related restaurants, allowing people to both get and satisfy the munchies at the same time!

318 FEELING NOT-SO-FRESH?

Cannabis has been put to many uses over the centuries, aside from the most obvious and popular one (that involves ignition and inhaling). There seems to be no end to the myriad helpful ways this particular plant can be of service to humanity, as evidenced by the folks at a company called Foria, who make marijuana-based vaginal suppositories for "extreme relief during menstruation." And if that sounds uncomfortable, don't worry. They also sell marijuana-based lube.

319 "I'D LIKE MY PAYCHECK IN QUARTERS, PLEASE."

Pot smokers often get saddled with the stereotype of being lazy, and an American company called, fittingly, American Green appears to have reinforced it when they rolled out the world's first marijuana vending machine and called it the ZaZZZ. So far they can only be found in legal dispensaries, but who knows? The way things are going, you might soon see them in your employer's break room...and frankly, weed would actually be a healthier option than most of the crap that comes out of those things.

320 POT-BELLIED PIGS

Bacon is already delicious and pretty close to perfect, so it's hard to imagine anyone improving on the basic concept. But that hasn't stopped one farmer in the state of Washington from giving it his best shot—by feeding his pigs a steady diet of marijuana, though only the stems and leaves left from the harvest. The farmer sells cuts of "Pot Pig" in downtown Seattle, and at least one satisfied customer has described the product as "the best pork chop you've ever had." A professor at Washington State University's Department of Animal Sciences had a slightly different take on things, however: "Of all the crazy things I've seen in my 37-plus years, this is the dumbest thing I've ever seen in my life."

321 BUD BOOZE

It is widely known that you can infuse butter and oil with THC, but what many don't realize is that you can do the same with alcohol. Heating marijuana in the oven to release the THC and then soaking it in a high-alcohol spirit results in a potent alcohol/marijuana hybrid colloquially known as "Green Dragon."

322 COMIC BOOKS AND CANNABIS COLLIDE!

When one comic book fan (who also happened to be the owner of a vape shop) visited comic conventions, he found himself organizing his entire schedule around getting high. Eventually it dawned on him that things would surely be easier if cannabis consumption was built right into the festivities. And thus, Chromic Con was born. So now every year, connoisseurs of both superheroes and skunkweed can enjoy the best of both worlds, with the minor drawback of having to deal with lingering odors in your cosplay ensemble.

323 NOT YOUR FATHER'S FAIR... WELL MAYBE, IF HE WAS A STONER

You know weed's gone mainstream when the county fair starts judging buds like prize pigs and blue-ribbon sheep. A fair in Colorado recently had a "Pot Pavilion," and some of the featured "highlights" included such twenty-one-and-over fare as "speed joint rolling" and a "Doritos-eating contest." We can probably assume that it won't be long until someone figures out how to deep-fry the stuff and put it on a stick.

324 HEDONISM RESORTS
HAVE NOTHING ON THIS

If vacation at a bed-and-breakfast makes you at all paranoid about who exactly you'll be living with for the weekend, you probably should avoid Get High Getaways in Denver. Husband-and-wife duo Dale Dyke and Chastity Osborn even include free marijuana-infused treats when you stay with them. One thing to note before you book your trip, however: Get High Getaway is described as "textile optional" so you may see more naked people just walking around than you intended.

325 WEED KEEPS
ELECTRIC COMPANIES
IN BUSINESS

While indoor marijuana growers make up a very small percentage of the US population, they account for an astronomical amount of energy consumption. Annually, they consume enough electricity to power two million American homes, approximately 1 percent of the annual consumption for the entire country. Most of this energy use comes from high-intensity grow lights, which are approximately five hundred times stronger than a reading lamp.

326 KUSH TOURISM

Do you like taking vacations, but wish the sightseeing experience could be a bit more...weed-oriented? If that's the case, then "kush tourism" might be just the ticket. Your next visit to Seattle can now include a guided tour of a pot farm and visits to local cannabis outlets and glass blowers. Just be sure to be completely sober if you get talked into attending one of those time-share seminars.

327 FACEBOOK FOR MARIJUANA

Ever wanted to show off your hand-blown glass bubbler to your stoner friends on *Facebook*, but didn't want your mom to see? There's an app for that. Mass-Roots (www.massroots.com), dubbed the "official social networking site for the stoner community," provides users with an outlet where they can share animated GIFs and pictures with other like-minded stoners. The site calls itself "an anonymous and independent social network built to connect medicinal cannabis patients." The app does not require identifying information like a name or email address from its users.

328 POT PURVEYORS UNITE

The first American Cannabis Business Summit happened in 2014 in Denver. A full eight hundred people were in attendance at the gathering, which provided a "national stage to discuss best practices and business developments from around the industry." This certainly sounds more interesting than your average business convention.

329 SMELL THE BURN

Going to the gym can be a nerve-racking experience when you're just starting out at a new place. So wouldn't it be nice to be able to light one up in the locker room without all the hassle of, you know, getting kicked out and possibly arrested? So goes the thinking of one gym owner in California, whose business, Power Plant (get it?) Fitness, opened in 2016 as the "world's first cannabis gym."

 NO MORE TROLLING
CRAIGSLIST FOR DEALERS

In the old days, you had to know a guy who knew a guy who knew a guy in order to score some pot. Today, there's Weedmaps. Based on Google's popular Google Maps service, Weedmaps pinpoints dispensaries and provides reviews and rankings to help you sort through the results. The site also helps users find licensed physicians and even provides suggestions on strains to use for particular ailments.

 SPACE OUT
TECHNOLOGY

The Herbalizer is the only vaporizer crafted by former NASA engineers. Inventors Josh Young and Bob Pratt took the knowledge they had gained from designing advanced NASA computer systems and used it to create a vaporizer that heats up in less than five seconds. It can be used with an inflatable bag, a simple hose, or as a classic aromatherapy system. Unlike many vaporizers, which have preset temperatures, the Herbalizer allows users to customize their heat settings between 143°C and 230°C.

332 FUN WITH GANJASAURUSES

Dinosaurs Smoking Weed probably isn't really a book for children, but it sure looks like one. As one might surmise, it's filled with illustrations of dinosaurs toking it up, along with plenty of "fun facts" about the creatures in question (like whether they prefer bongs or joints). Oh, and it comes with crayons, because it's a coloring book.

 HIGH ART

Not all museums are boring repositories of stodginess. The Oakland Museum of California held an exhibit in 2016 called *Altered State: Marijuana in California*, with the intention of encouraging dialogue about the controversial plant. It was probably a good idea to focus on that and not the local weed-inspired art, because there are only so many times you can look at a frog playing a flute next to a purple river filled with narwhals.

 THE GREEN LADY

In apparent support of New York's recent passage of the limited legalization of medical marijuana, *The New York Times* ran its very first ad for weed. Sadly, it wasn't an ad for the Vapor Pimp in Arizona, but "a congratulatory note from a Seattle start-up" that touted the benefits of cannabis's healing abilities.

335 A PIPE CAN BE A WORK OF ART

Jason Harris, a glassblower, was a bong-maker extraordinaire and owner of Jerome Baker Designs. His designs are widely considered works of art by weed connoisseurs and are a favorite of celebrity tokers. Even small bongs can start at $150 a pop, especially after a law enforcement raid temporarily shut down Harris's business in 2003, making his designs even more exclusive finds.

336 POT POLISH

If you're ever in California, possess a license to procure legal marijuana, and have around $65 in your pocket, a woman named Louisiana Pham will do your nails. With weed. No, you both don't smoke it up while she works (although that might be interesting to watch). What she does is take the customer's marijuana and work it into the polish for a unique, hemp-filled look. This may be the only way to get your weed over the border...

337 WAX ON, NOD OFF

If you've never heard of "marijuana wax," it's not what happens when you fall asleep with a joint behind your ear. It's a concentrated form of cannabis that's created by packing it tightly into a tube, and then blasting it with a butane torch. Apart from providing a quicker way to get high, it's reportedly also the strongest form of weed you can buy.

 ONE STOP SHOP

In January of 2016, the zoning commission in a town in Colorado approved construction for the world's first pot mini-mall. No less than five licenses were issued for separate marijuana retail businesses within the mall, which is probably the limit considering they needed to save space for a larger-than-average food court.

 CANNABIS THE BARBARIAN

When you're an artist who goes by the name Trek Thunder Kelly, chances are good that subtlety isn't your strong suit. The evidence appears to bear this out, as one of his works, titled *Going Green: Governator T-1000*, is a statue made out of $1,000 worth of marijuana in the vague shape of Arnold Schwarzenegger.

340 BUT HOW DOES IT PERFORM ON EMISSIONS TESTS?

An American inventor claims to have realized the dream of Cheech and Chong fans everywhere and made a car out of hemp. Calling his $200,000 prototype the "Cannabis Car," he believes it will be an important weapon against climate change. If you're feeling green (and optimistic), he's taking orders, and prices range from $40,000 for a 130-horsepower model to $197,000 for something a bit fancier. A dash-mounted hookah, maybe?

341 MAYBE YOU SHOULDN'T ASK SO MANY QUESTIONS, LITTLE GIRL

Among the many illustrated, pot-related children's books you might consider for a stocking stuffer this gift-giving season is *It's Just a Plant*. In this heart-warming tale, a young girl learns all about the wonders of marijuana from Mom and Dad, as well as ancillary characters like a farmer, a doctor, and a police officer. Whether or not any Phish roadies living nearby felt offended by not being included is unknown at this time.

342 LIGHTING UP

Artist Bentley Meeker showcased an exhibition at New York City's National Arts Club in 2015. As a sculptor of glass and light, his intention was to show the viewer how little of the full light spectrum is contained in LED lights compared to halogen. Included in his exhibition was a chandelier made out of hand-blown glass bongs he called *The Bongolier*.

343 DUTCH TREAT

For a little less than $15, you can purchase a Netherlands-produced pack of Cannadoms, which are exactly what the title probably made you think they are: cannabis-flavored condoms. Of course this comes from the land of "coffee" shops and red-light districts.

344 EASEL RIDER

There's been plenty of art created while the artist was high, but few actually make portraits using pot smoke as their medium. Fernando de La Rocque is a painter from Brazil who blows a lungful of the cannabis he's inhaled through a stencil over paper, creating "golden-hued" images that require around a week (and five joints) to complete.

345 I GUESS "RODNEY THE RED-EYED RACCOON" WAS TAKEN

Children's books that touch on the subject of marijuana aren't so much a cause for outrage as they might have been twenty years ago. However, knowing there's a franchise called *Stinky Steve Explains* might make even the most pro-pot parent raise an eyebrow. Thankfully, the eponymous Steve isn't just a stereotypical stoner, but a cartoon skunk that teaches kids about all sorts of weed-related issues. Some sample titles include *Stinky Steve Explains Casual Cannabis* and *Stinky Steve Explains Daddy's Dabs*.

346 NO SURPRISES HERE

Comedians and pot icons Cheech and Chong are no strangers to the social media revolution. In fact, they have over two million followers on their Instagram page, which is mostly filled with exactly what you'd expect: weed and memes.

347 AT LEAST HE'S HONEST

One of the works of performance artist Chris Burden was something he called *Coals to Newcastle*, which is British slang for "a pointless act." He attached American-grown marijuana, rolled into joints, to model airplanes, which he flew over the border from California to Mexico. Emblazoned on the sides of the planes were phrases such as "Hecho en U.S.A." and "Fumen los Muchachos!" (loose translations: "Made in U.S.A." and "Smoke up, dudes!").

348 CHUBBY TOKERS UNITE

Noted comedian/actor/cannabis enthusiast Seth Rogen's influence on the film industry cannot be denied. Case in point, when working on *Zack and Miri Make a Porno* with Rogen, director Kevin Smith stated that merely being in Rogen's presence inspired him to start smoking more marijuana, and eventually become, in his words, a stoner.

349 NOW TO FIND TWO STONER TWINS FOR THE AD CAMPAIGN

It sounds like a gimmick, but a company called AXIM Biotechnologies has developed a cannabis chewing gum. Not for getting high, as it actually contains just a small amount of psychotropic ingredients (5 milligrams), but for treating multiple sclerosis patients. The goal was to make a delivery system for pain-relief medicine that was socially acceptable, tasty, and free from adverse side effects, and according to the company chief, "chewing gum meets all these criteria."

350 GREEN VIBRATIONS

Sex toys can take a lot of different shapes and sizes, but people who yearned to pleasure themselves with a polymer-based marijuana leaf have historically been neglected. Until now, that is. A woman named Heather Schnurr has finally created a vibrator to fill that niche, so to speak, and named it the Mary Jane Vibrator.

 351 PIXELATED POTHEADS

The Saints Row series of video games are famous for doing everything in their power to be even more outrageous than the Grand Theft Auto franchise. In the game, you can openly purchase marijuana, smoke it via blunt or bong, and get treated to a barrage of weed puns from the vendor as you make your purchase. And after you consume the product, the screen glazes over in a smoky haze.

 352 IT DOESN'T NEED TO GET YOU HIGH

Marijuana has a number of medical benefits, and also has the fortunate side effect of getting the patient high. But for patients who want to treat their lower back pain without the psychedelic bonus, there's hope. Researchers at an Israeli medical marijuana company have developed a strain called Avidekel, which contains almost no THC but is packed full of cannabidiol (CBD), a chemical very similar to THC that possesses anti-inflammatory properties without THC's euphoric side effects.

353 A BONG WITH A DONG

In a classic example of no one stopping to ask "Why?" an online sex toy company called Pipedreams created the "Peter Piper" dildo/smoking device. It's, um, basically just what it sounds like: a sex toy with a bowl on it. Described on the packaging as the "8-inch Pecker Puffer," it encourages the customer to "Smoke it, then poke it!"

354 BAKED BRANDING

Most people have heard of the classic sativa strain with the catchy name of "Maui Wowie." But as far as creative monikers for marijuana strains go, it's actually pretty tame. Names of strains can get pretty creative, such as "Hippie Chicken," "Electric Kool-Aid," and "Alien Asshat."

355 CORPORATE CANNABIS

Big companies have historically been shy about aligning themselves with the marijuana legalization movement. But as medical and recreational marijuana rapidly make strides toward public acceptability, some have seen the benefits of offering their support. One of the biggest corporations in existence, Microsoft, recently got on board by stating their intention to produce plant-tracking software for marijuana growers. Sorry if you were hoping they announced more video games designed specifically for stoners.

356 THE SEX BONG

We've already discussed the delicate matter of "Peter Piper," the dildo/bong. This next thing is...sort of that, but just a little different. Different in that where the Peter Piper is used in different circumstances at different times, this as-yet-unnamed contraption lets you engage in both acts simultaneously. So far it's only in the patent stage, but, if created, it promises to "generate stimulatory vibrations" while you smoke from it.

357 THE ORIGINAL
CANNABIS CAR

Not only was Henry Ford's first Model T car made to run on ethanol made from hemp, but much of the car itself was made from plastic panels made from hemp fibers. Ford claimed that the panels had ten times the impact strength of steel panels. He believed that "apples, weeds, sawdust—almost anything" could be made into fuel and sought to explore those options further. Unfortunately, this did not happen, because of the easy operation of gasoline engines, the abundance of petroleum from new oil field discoveries, and pressure from the petroleum industry to keep itself the main supplier of fuel. Alternative fuels only became seriously researched more than fifty years later when environmental concerns spurred more attention to the matter.

358 THE SECRET
IN MY PANTS

For the fashionably discreet, the Buckle Puffer is a marijuana pipe disguised as a belt buckle. Made of machine-cut, nickel-plated aluminum, it doesn't reek after use due to its "glove-like fit," and looks rather decent when housed in its covert belt form.

359 COVERT CANNABIS

While it's still in the prototype stage, the Royght! stealth bong takes sneakiness to a new level by providing an adapter that fits over a disposable cup, the sort you might buy at McDonald's or Starbucks. It's basically a portable bong that makes it look like the only drug you're guzzling down is caffeine.

360 WAKE UP HEMP-FRESH

Just in case the crappy presents you get Dad every year aren't quite stinky enough, one option is Dope on a Rope Soap. It's just like those twine-attached, cheap-cologne-infused soaps of yesteryear, only with, you know, weed inside of it. He might get some weird looks at the office and an uncomfortable meeting with his boss if he starts using it every day, however.

361 FINALLY, A WAY TO MAKE ROB SCHNEIDER MOVIES WATCHABLE

The Scarlet Theater in Colorado is looking to fill its own unique niche in the brave new world of legalized marijuana by offering moviegoers the chance to smoke weed while enjoying an indie or cult classic film. Plans include a "world class" restaurant onsite, along with a "BYOC" (assuming the "C" is for "cannabis," not "candy") lounge with plenty of "apparatuses."

362 DANK DISH PIZZA

How has nobody ever thought of this before? A designer in New York City named Nikolas Gregory has developed a pizza box that has a small square you can tear out to make the entire thing a pipe, and a stand in the middle that serves as a bowl. Getting one delivered in thirty minutes or less from a pie joint full of weed enthusiasts might be a tall order, though.

363 WEED CAN LEAD YOU TO TRUE LOVE

It seems there's a niche dating site for every group of people imaginable, so it's no surprise that there's even one for lovelorn stoners. Similar to sites like Match.com and OkCupid.com, 420Singles.com bills itself as a "cannabis dating site and social network for marijuana enthusiasts."

364 I NOW PRONOUNCE YOU HIGH AND STONED

Since legalizing weed, the state of Colorado has seen a number of pot-related elements being incorporated into weddings, such as vaping stations in place of open bars and cannabis leaf bouquets. As one wedding planner said, "With it being legal in Colorado, it's not surprising to hear that some couples are planning to incorporate it into their day." Plus, the Chicken Dance can finally be enjoyed with the enthusiasm it deserves.

365 PRESUMABLY POT BROWNIES ON THE DESSERT MENU?

A company based in Washington State called MagicalButter has been operating a mobile food truck for a while now, but recently it decided to expand its business by opening an actual restaurant. As far as the fare they'll be offering to hungry customers, the menu includes "high-end everyday foods." And as you may have guessed from their unorthodox name, all dishes are prepared with THC-infused cheese, oil, and butter.

366 JAVA CON GANJA

If you're ever in Los Angeles and need some morning joe before an important meeting, you should probably avoid ordering the coffee made with "heirloom Ethiopian Yirgacheffe 'Zero Defect' coffee beans," sold by a coffee shop called Compelling & Rich. That word salad of an ingredient not only smells like the stinkiest of weed, it *is* weed. The owner has come up with some complicated way of combining marijuana with the beans (no, he isn't just plopping buds into the roaster), and apparently it's all perfectly legal.

SEVEN

HISTORICAL HEMP

Given that humans have been making use of cannabis since we were first learning to both hunt and gather at the same time, and we weren't even a country until 1867, the Great White North's contributions to marijuana history are more recent. But the lessons of the past are important for anyone wishing to know more about the plants they're smoking, vaping, or baking into pastry. So here's your opportunity to properly edify yourself on the age-old story of our planet's most entertaining plant. Starting with...

367 THERE'S A REASON THOSE STATUES LOOK DAZED

Scientists have long been puzzled as to exactly how those giant rock figures on Easter Island got there. One controversial theory, which was tested out by volunteers, is that hemp was a major part of the process. No, the ancient folks didn't smoke it for artistic inspiration, but rather used it as rope to "walk" the monoliths to their current location.

368 COLD WAR CANNABIS

During the Cold War, the US Army experimented with giving soldiers and citizens synthetic marijuana (among other things) in an attempt to weaponize what is normally thought to be a quite peaceful herb. Ultimately, they concluded that psychoactive drugs "were either too unpredictable or too mellow to be useful as weapons." That's unfortunate, since the whole mess in the Middle East could probably be cleared up in a weekend if we found a way to take out ISIS while they were all sitting around watching *SpongeBob SquarePants* reruns.

369 MARY JANE AT MONTICELLO

The third US president, Thomas Jefferson, is sometimes quoted as saying, "Some of my finest hours have been spent on my back veranda, smoking hemp, and observing as far as my eye can see." But according to the caretakers of his estate, while Jefferson did indeed grow marijuana (and the possibility of him occasionally partaking in it is certainly high), he never said any such thing.

370 ANCIENT WONDERS

Medical marijuana isn't a new idea. It actually appears in one of the oldest medical guides ever found, *De Materia Medica*, by Pedanius Dioscorides, a medic in the Roman army. He cites cannabis as a great way to lessen inflammation and heal earaches.

371 DANGER IN THE WEEDS

While fighting the Taliban in Afghanistan in 2006, the chief of the Canadian defense staff at the time, Rick Hillier, reported a rather unusual problem: the enemy was using "forests" of marijuana as cover, and one of the insurgents had even covered an entire car in cannabis leaves. To address this unforeseen complication, it was decided to burn the entire area down. But that turned out to create a whole new set of conundrums, as Hillier explained: "A couple of brown plants on the edges of some of those [forests] did catch on fire. But a section of soldiers that was downwind from that had some ill effects and decided that was probably not the right course of action."

372 THE ORIGINAL DR. FEELGOOD

Dr. William O'Shaughnessy of Ireland is widely regarded as the father of modern medicine. Modern cannabis medicine, that is. Plying his trade in the 1800s, he discovered the pain-relieving qualities of marijuana while working for the British East India Company and popularized its use in England and America. It seems a shame that few people recognize his accomplishments, while his fellow countryman Arthur Guinness gets all the glory simply for brewing some beer.

373 THE CANNABIS QUEEN

England's Queen Victoria (of the, you know, Victorian Era) bucked the uptight norms of the day via her marijuana use. Well, not really. Her doctor actually prescribed it to her to relieve the agony brought on by menstrual cramps. She probably didn't even smoke it. So, let's not dwell on the specifics involved in the "treatment."

374 HORRIBLE HARRY

A man named Harry Anslinger has the dubious distinction of being the father of America's undeclared war on marijuana. Back in the 1930s, he was the head of the Federal Bureau of Narcotics, which would eventually become the US Drug Enforcement Agency. He led a personal crusade against musicians with a fondness for weed, and orchestrated countless raids while ordering his men to "shoot first."

375 "WHEREFORE ART THOU MY BELOVED ONE-HITTER?"

An excavation of William Shakespeare's garden yielded a bumper crop. Archaeologists found four-hundred-year-old smoking pipes, and forensic testing showed they contained trace amounts of marijuana. And while there's no irrefutable evidence that the Bard partook in the hedonistic herb, it may go a long way in explaining quotes like this one from *Julius Caesar*:

> "Is Brutus sick? And is it physical
> To walk unbraced and suck up the humours
> Of the dank morning?"

376 HOLY CRACKPOT CRUSADERS!

The war on marijuana in the mid-1900s saw a lot of hyperbole on the part of the authorities, who were determined to stamp out the "menace" of the devil weed. A good example of this was when Dr. James Munch, a pharmacologist, stated the following while serving as an expert witness for the government: "After two puffs on a marijuana cigarette, I was turned into a bat." Munch's testimony was frequently so silly that many of the resulting jail sentences were later reduced.

377 THE ALL-PURPOSE HERB

The ancient Egyptians were no strangers to the healing powers of marijuana, and had all sorts of cannabis-related medical cures. Archaeologists have found scrolls describing treatments for everything from toenail injuries to female "inflammation" woes, the latter achieved by mixing herbs with honey and putting them into women's vaginas.

FUNNY HATS
OPTIONAL?

Back in the mid-1800s, famous French creative types like Charles Baudelaire, Alexandre Dumas, and Victor Hugo met in secret to get their hashish on, and formed the rather unimaginatively named club called Club des Hachichins. They really got into it—dressing in Arabic clothing and drinking strong foreign coffees in between pulls from the hookah. Whether this practice helped with their art is open to debate, but in Baudelaire's case, it certainly brought out his air for the dramatic: "At first, a certain absurd, irresistible hilarity overcomes you. The most ordinary words, the simplest ideas assume a new and bizarre aspect. This mirth is intolerable to you; but it is useless to resist. The demon has invaded you…"

HIGH
TEA

According to legend, Shen Neng of China saw the merits of medicinal Mary Jane potentially as early as around 2700 B.C.E. He was known to prescribe cannabis tea for treating ailments like gout, rheumatism, and malaria. We have no way of knowing how successful his cures were, but it seems slightly doubtful that he had much success with the other affliction he gave people his special tea for: memory loss.

HOLY
HASH

380

The very first recorded mention of marijuana comes from India when it was written down in the collection of holy books known as the Vedas. They say that the god Shiva "took pity on humans and brought cannabis from the Himalayas to give health and pleasure," and praised cannabis for its ability to relieve stress. This reverence for marijuana remains true for many in India to this very day. Giving everyone free weed seems like a surprisingly nice thing to do, seeing as we're talking about a blue god with three eyes whose purported goal is to destroy the universe.

PETTICOATS AND
HASH PIPES

381

Turkish hashish first made its appearance in the United States during the 1876 World's Fair in Philadelphia, when Sultan Abdülaziz I set up a pavilion filled with hookahs and the products to go in said hookahs. Reportedly, this pavilion was the first place visited by many of the attendees, which certainly must have made the rest of the attractions at the fair way, way more interesting.

382 THE ORIGIN OF "420"

So, why do we associate the number "420" with marijuana? Some will tell you it's a police code, a reference to a Bob Dylan song, or maybe it's the birthday of Germany's least-mellow stoner, Adolf Hitler. But the most likely reason is that this was the scheduled time a group of high-school students in Marin County, California, would habitually meet by a statue of Louis Pasteur in order to indulge their cannabis cravings in the early 1970s. They were known as the Waldos, and one of them was friends with a member of the yet-to-be-world-famous Grateful Dead. The group started using "420" as slang for getting high, and the rest is history.

383 WEED SPAWNED L.A.'S GREATEST PRANK

On the day California's relaxed marijuana law took effect in January 1976, artist and marijuana advocate Danny Finegood modified one of the state's most famous landmarks to commemorate the event. Using a series of curtains, he changed the beloved Hollywood sign to read "Hollyweed." The prank even earned him an A for a school assignment.

384 REEFER MADNESS, INDEED!

"Reefer" is another name for a marijuana cigarette. The name is thought to have derived from the Spanish word for marijuana: *grifa*. You don't have to be high to know that sounds funny since the word "marijuana" was Spanish in the first place, but it's true. "Reefer" is now one of the most common terms for the drug.

385 HOLY HERB

The Cannaterian Church, otherwise known as the First Church of Cannabis, boasts more than a thousand adherents globally and has official federal recognition from the United States as a religious organization. Despite some pushback from the local police force, the first service went off with great fanfare, including a comedian, live music, and dancing. If you're looking to join, make sure you bring your monthly dues: $4.20.

 ## KILLER
BONG

During the later stages of the Vietnam War, many US soldiers smoked the locally grown marijuana to deal with the stress and boredom. In 1970, a documentary crew filmed a squad leader named Vito, who showed off "Ralph," a 12-gauge shotgun repurposed as a pipe. A similar scene was later shot by film director and Vietnam War veteran Oliver Stone in his movie *Platoon*.

 ## BONGS BEFORE
BATTLE

Pot isn't always about peace and love. The Zulus and other African tribes like the Sothos regularly smoked marijuana before going forth into battle. Famed explorer David Livingstone recorded how they "sat down and smoked [hemp] in order that they might make an effective onslaught."

388 BHANG, BHANG, YOU'RE DEAD

"Bhang" is a traditional Indian preparation of marijuana as a drink for consumption, and has been used for hundreds of years in both food and drink. One use for bhang was for steeling soldiers' nerves during war. For example, when the troops of Gobind Singh, the founder of Sikhism, became terrified by the sight of an approaching elephant during a battle, Singh chose one man to go forth and slay the beast. After the man was prepared with a bit of bhang (along with a little opium), Singh accomplished the deed and his fellow soldiers were inspired to rally and win the day. Sikhs celebrate the anniversary of this event by, you guessed it, drinking bhang.

389 THE POWER OF KUSH COMPELS YOU!

Hemp was a very important part of many aspects of everyday life in ancient China. In addition to serving as a source of clothing, paper, and medicine, it also found its way into some other...unorthodox uses. For example, they carved cannabis stalks into snakes and waved them around in order to dispel demons from those who they believed were possessed.

390 WEED, THE HEAVENLY, JOYGIVING SKYFLIER

At the end of the nineteenth century, an official group called the Indian Hemp Drugs Commission was charged with studying the use and prohibition feasibility of marijuana and bhang in India. The rather flowery conclusion they came to was this: "Bhang is the Joygiver, the Skyflier, the Heavenly-Guide, the Poor Man's Heaven, the Soother of Grief....No god or man is as good as the religious drinker of bhang.... The supporting power of bhang has brought many a Hindu family safe through the miseries of famine. To forbid or even seriously to restrict the use of so holy and gracious an herb as the hemp would cause widespread suffering and annoyance and, to large bands of worshipped ascetics, deep-seated anger."

391 RELIC OF THE STONED AGE

A 2,400- to 2,800-year-old corpse was found recently in China, surrounded in death by an "extraordinary cache" of cannabis plants. The marijuana was arranged meticulously, as if it were intended to be a shroud. Forensics determined that the man was Caucasian, around the age of thirty-five when he died, and likely a shaman of some sort. Willie Nelson was presumably pleased to finally find closure at the discovery of his long-lost ancestor.

392 NAZIS AND WEED

One's first instinct would be to suppose that the Nazi government of the 1930s was extra harsh toward anyone caught possessing or selling marijuana. It's actually kind of the opposite, but not because they were nice guys or anything. It's just that hardly anyone in Germany at the time even knew what it was, and the police were generally befuddled whenever foreign workers were caught smoking it. In fact, it wasn't until around the late 1960s that law enforcement started dealing with it seriously.

393 ANCIENT TOKERS

Back in 1929, a Russian archaeologist was exploring some ancient ruins in an area between Siberia and Mongolia when he found a trench containing the centuries-old corpses of several horses and one embalmed man. In the vicinity was a cauldron containing burnt marijuana seeds, hemp clothing, and censers (burning devices) used for cannabis inhalation. What they determined from all this is that the evidence of pot smoking had nothing to do with religion, but was merely a normal activity for this man's culture at the time.

GREEN EQUINE
LIDOCAINE

The ancient Greeks, like the Chinese and various other cultures, used cannabis to treat all manner of human illnesses. But they didn't limit their treatments to their fellow man. They also saw the veterinary possibilities, and reportedly rubbed it on their horses to heal their wounds after battle. Which at least probably helped calm their stress from being put in that position in the first place.

I SEE
STONED PEOPLE

Ancient China wasn't always pro-marijuana. When Taoism began to take over around the year 600 B.C.E., weed was condemned because they saw it as debilitating and believed it made people see demons. Eventually, however, as people experimented with cannabis seeds, they changed their minds about the hallucinogenic qualities and decided they may provide a positive way to commune with ghosts and achieve immortality. It's a shame that pot can't really do all those things, but it might be a fun way to scare a gullible person at a party.

 396 A LONG, STRANGE TRIP

It's believed that marijuana showed up in the Middle East somewhere between 1000 and 2000 B.C.E., and was introduced to the region by the nomadic (and pot-loving) Scythians. The plant subsequently made its way to places like Russia and Ukraine, then to Europe through the efforts of Germanic tribes, eventually to England, and finally into the hands of Russell Brand.

397 THE LAND OF
THE RISING BUD

Like China, ancient Japan found myriad uses for the cannabis plant. In addition to being burned to ward off evil spirits, marijuana was also a part of marriage proceedings—hung inside the home or on surrounding trees to ensure a lover's fidelity.

398 ORIGIN OF THE
ZIG ZAG MAN

Have you even wondered who that swarthy rapscallion is on the cover of Zig Zag rolling paper packages? Well, as legend has it, he's an unnamed French soldier (or "Zouave") who fought during the Siege of Sevastopol during the Crimean War. When his pipe was shattered by a bullet, he allegedly came up with the idea of rolling up a cigarette using the paper from a gunpowder bag.

399 BURIED PLEASURE

When a power company in Russia was putting up some power lines, they inadvertently uncovered several 2,400-year-old Scythian relics made out of pure gold. It's believed that said relics were used by tribal chiefs as inhalation devices for cannabis and opium. In other words, they found the world's oldest bongs.

400 OUR ANCESTORS GOT HIGH ALL THE TIME

During the recent excavation of a 2,700-year-old gravesite, a cache of nearly two pounds of pot was discovered. Tests performed on the ancient stash found it to be very similar chemically to the variety grown today, and to possess the same psychoactive properties. This cast doubt on the notion that ancient civilizations grew hemp plants strictly for making clothing and rope. Scientists believe the plant matter was ingested rather than smoked, as they found no apparatus necessary for smoking it.

WHY "BONG"?

The origin of the word "bong" is from the Thai language. They also say *bong*, or *buang*, to refer to a cylinder made from wood or bamboo that's used for smoking. *Buang* can also refer to "the hole for inserting the handle into a metal toolhead," so just be aware so you don't run into any conundrums at the Phuket Home Depot.

SUBTLE TITLE

Around the time of the infamous anti-pot film *Reefer Madness* came another bit of cinematic silliness called *Assassin of Youth*. In it, a journalist goes undercover as a soda jerk in order to observe a marijuana gang. The main message in this film is how the word "assassin" is derived from "hashish" (which is actually true), and so obviously marijuana's sole purpose is to incite people to murder, and the plant is only good for "exciting the basest and most criminal tendencies in the minds of its addicts" (which is actually not true).

403 THE SCOURGE OF THE LOCOWEED

Back in the days when marijuana was public enemy number one, newspapers felt free to let loose with exaggeration and fear mongering, resulting in reports like this one, from a 1915 edition of the *Ogden Standard-Examiner* in Utah: "If a limit of one cigarette were set, no great lasting harm might come to the indulger, but in order to keep up the feeling of elation, another and perhaps another of the paper-wrapped poison is consumed, until the victim is in a state of wild frenzy. When in this condition, he often goes on a rampage that brings death to whoever crosses his path. The period of temporary insanity lasts for several hours and is followed by the victim falling into a deep sleep that lasts 24 hours or more. He awakes with no knowledge of what has transpired while the full effects of the drug were upon him. It takes only a few months of constant indulgence in the cigarette habit to bring on permanent insanity."

THE ZTORY OF ZIG ZAGS

404

Zig Zag rolling papers were invented in 1894 by the Braunstein brothers, after developing an ingenious packaging process (that's used to this very day) that allowed for one paper to be pulled from the package via a simple tug. The interweaving way the papers were cut led to the wacky name of the product, and so impressed the judges at the 1900 Exposition Universelle in Paris that the brothers were awarded a gold medal. Whether the brothers snuck a little something extra into the tobacco to sway the judges is open to debate.

SO, WHEN ARE THOSE STUDIES WRAPPING UP?

405

In 1970, Dr. Roger O. Egeberg, the US assistant secretary of health, recommended that since the scientists at the time didn't know enough about marijuana, the United States should continue to ban it "until the completion of certain studies now underway to resolve the issue." Apparently the research is still ongoing, as it is still banned in the United States. You do have to admire just how much intense and exacting the research must be, seeing as how it's been going on for decades now.

406 THE DOOBFATHER

Raphael Mechoulam is an organic chemist from Israel whose work on marijuana earned him the title "the patriarch of cannabis science." Starting in the early 1960s, Mechoulam toiled away in search of the mysteries to be found in weed, and he was the one who first discovered that it was THC that made the plant a whole lot more fun than, say, a dandelion or whatever.

407 NO NEED FOR JELLY

Back in medieval times people ate hash brownies too, or at least a reasonable facsimile thereof. What they would do is scrounge up some poppies, hemp, and whatever the heck darnel is (it's a type of grass), then mash it all together to make something they called "crazy bread." Just in case you were wondering why history professors always giggle when eating appetizers at Little Caesars.

 GROW IT OR ELSE

Before America made marijuana *herba non grata* (we're talking the seventeenth century here), the government actually required farmers to grow hemp for important things like sails, rope, and garments. It was even considered legal tender in a few states. The system apparently worked well enough, although surely it must have caused quite a mess in colonial-era strip clubs.

 BLOOD ON THE PRAIRIE

Reefer Madness wasn't the only insane anti-pot movie from the early part of the last century. Another entry in the ridiculous pantheon is *High on the Range*, which tells the story of Dave the rancher. After smoking less than one entire joint, he goes on a drug-fueled murder rampage. We're lucky there wasn't any PCP in that joint, which presumably would have led to the deaths of millions.

410 THE ROAD TO
GIGGLING PERDITION

Another *Reefer Madness*–era example of Hollywood anti-pot lunacy is a straightforwardly titled film called *Marihuana*, which claimed to be "divulging heretofore unheard of orgies of youths' dissipation." In it, after a group of the aforementioned innocent youths goes skinny-dipping after smoking some "giggle weed," one of them inexplicably becomes a weed-dealing kingpin and goes on a violent crime spree.

411 CHINESE
CHEEBA

China has been experimenting with the medicinal aspects of marijuana for the past five thousand years or so and, now that the plant is becoming less taboo worldwide, the nation is positioning itself to be a global leader in the cannabis trade. Over half of all patents concerning pot belong to China now, according to the World Intellectual Property Organization.

412 WEED + WINE = BEST MEDICINE EVER

China's first surgeon was a man named Hua Tuo, who was considered a "miracle doctor" for his ability to accidentally kill people slightly less often than other doctors of the time. He was also the first physician to use cannabis as an anesthetic, grinding it into powder and mixing it with wine, thereby making anyone who tells you that you should never mix weed with alcohol look like a damn fool.

413 VIVA LA COCKROACH

The origin of the word "roach," meaning the leftover part of a joint after it's been smoked, comes from Mexico, where the word for cockroach is *cucaracha*. And if you recognize that word from the old folk song, "La Cucaracha," that's very appropriate since that song is totally filled with weed references, and *tabaco de cucaracha* is a slang term for low-grade cannabis.

THE WORM
TURNS

Marijuana has played a major part in cultures all around the world, often becoming central to their myths and legends. Take, for example, this tale from Japan: There were once two women who were both weavers of hemp. One woman made fine hemp fabric but was slow. Her neighbor made coarse fabric but worked quickly. During market days, it was customary for Japanese women to dress their best, and the two women began to weave new dresses. The woman who worked quickly had her dress ready on time, but it wasn't fashionable. Her neighbor only managed to get the unbleached white strands ready, and when market day came, she didn't have her dress ready. So, she persuaded her husband to carry her in a jar so only her neck, with the white hemp strands around it, would be visible. On the way to market, the woman in the jar saw her neighbor and started making fun of her coarse dress. The neighbor shot back that at least she was clothed. "Break the jar," she told everyone, "and you will find a naked woman." The husband became so mortified that he dropped the jar, which broke and revealed his naked wife clothed only in hemp strands around her neck. The woman was so ashamed she buried herself and turned into an earthworm. And that is why the earthworm has white rings around its neck.

415 POT PATOIS

Every generation has its own slang word for marijuana, with "weed" currently being the one that's most en vogue. It apparently rose to the top of the popularity chart in the 1990s, when young people wanted to get away from the "grass" their parents smoked or the "dope" their grandparents appropriated from African-American lingo in the 1930s. We can only hope that "hippie lettuce" will be making a comeback in the near future.

416 DOPE ROPE

Although it's impossible to mark exactly when hemp was first used to make rope, historians estimate that early man wove hemp ropes and fastened bamboo together to make floating rafts—so, yeah, that's a long time ago. Before all of the synthetic stuff that we use today was created, rafts, pulleys, and fishnets were likely all fashioned from hemp seed. If you're interested in learning more about the history of hemp rope, you can find more information in local and national maritime museums. Smoke a joint and join the museum tour; those museum tour guides will never seem so cool.

417 POT PAPER— THEN AND NOW

Hemp paper has a long and storied history—some people say America's Declaration of Independence was drafted on hemp paper! Whether you believe this theory or not, hemp paper is still around today and thus we need to consider how to use pot paper in our current lives. Forget all-natural stationery and recyclable schoolbooks: roll up your best roach with some hemp sheet and write your own history (seriously, write it down 'cause you might forget it).

418 YOU CAN BE PIOUS BY SMOKING WEED!

Though many devoutly religious men and women deny that pot had a place in the Bible, an alternative etymological theory presented by workers at the Hebrew University of Jerusalem says otherwise. They say that the word "cannabis" actually comes from the Arabic *kunnab*, which comes from the Syriac *qunnappa*, which came from the Hebrew *pannag*. They say that this explains that the *pannag* mentioned in the Bible (Ezekiel 27:17) would therefore be cannabis. Another phrase found in the Bible, "reed of balm," is also thought to translate to "cannabis," as it is rendered in traditional Hebrew as *kannabos* or *kannabus*.

419 GIVE WAR A CHANCE

During World War II, the American government actually requested that more people grow hemp. The country's supply of hemp boat rigging and canvas had previously come from the South Pacific, but as much of this territory was now in the hands of the Japanese, the supply was running low. The US government created a film called *Hemp for Victory* to educate farmers on the need for hemp and how to grow it. The government distributed four hundred thousand pounds of cannabis seeds to farmers, who in turn produced forty-two thousand tons of hemp per year until 1946.

420 YOU PROBABLY WOULD TELL THE TRUTH

War on Drugs? How about War with Drugs? During World War II, the Office of Strategic Services (the predecessor to America's infamous Central Intelligence Agency) used marijuana to force the truth from captives. As odd as it sounds, the OSS reported that once intoxicated, the captive was "loquacious and free in his impartation of information." How the OSS managed to get the captive to recall anything useful without giggling is as of yet unknown. Perhaps the CIA will leak those documents in the future.